# Bernard Bailyn

# TO BEGIN THE WORLD ANEW

Bernard Bailyn did his undergraduate work at Williams College and his graduate work at Harvard, where he is currently Adams University Professor Emeritus and director of the International Seminar on the Atlantic World. His previous books include *The New England Merchants in the Seventeenth Century*; *Education in the Forming of American Society*; *Pamphlets of the American Revolution, 1750–1776*; *The Ideological Origins of the American Revolution*, which received the Pulitzer and Bancroft Prizes in 1968; *The Ordeal of Thomas Hutchinson*, which won the 1975 National Book Award for History; *Voyagers to the West*, which won the Pulitzer Prize in 1987; and *Faces of Revolution: Personalities and Themes in the Struggle for American Independence*.

D0311182

# TO BEGIN THE WORLD ANEW

## The Genius and Ambiguities
## of the American Founders

**BERNARD BAILYN**

*For Richard
and Anne
Jim + Anstice*

VINTAGE BOOKS

A DIVISION OF RANDOM HOUSE, INC.

NEW YORK

FIRST VINTAGE BOOKS EDITION, FEBRUARY 2004

*Copyright © 2003 by Bernard Bailyn*

All rights reserved under International and Pan-American Copyright Conventions.
Published in the United States by Vintage Books, a division of Random House, Inc.,
New York, and simultaneously in Canada by Random House of Canada Limited,
Toronto. Originally published in hardcover in the United States by Alfred A. Knopf,
a division of Random House, Inc., New York, in 2003.

The Library of Congress has cataloged the Knopf edition as follows:
Bailyn, Bernard
To begin the world anew: the genius and ambiguities of the American founders /
Bernard Bailyn.—1st ed.
p.   cm.
ISBN 0-375-41377-4
Includes bibliographical references and index.
1. United States—Politics and government—1775–1783.   2. United States—
Politics and government—1783–1809.   3. Statesmen—United States—History—
18th century.   4. Presidents—United States—History—18th century.
5. Revolutionaries—United States—History—18th century.
6. Constitutional history—United States.
I. Title.
E302.1.B16  2003
973.3—dc21       2002019020

**Vintage ISBN: 0-375-71308-5**

*Author photograph © Richard Feldman*
*Book design by Anthea Lingeman*

www.vintagebooks.com

Printed in the United States of America
10   9   8   7   6   5   4   3   2   1

# FOR LOTTE

## AND THE WOMEN OF FIVE GENERATIONS

# Contents

# Preface

These studies, though written over a period of years, have a unity of purpose and a consistency of theme. They are an attempt to probe aspects of the founding of the American nation through analysis of certain uniquely important people and documents and through study of the location, the context, of the Revolutionary generation in the greater world of which they were a part. That they were provincials—marginal, borderland people—in the broad context of eighteenth-century Euro-American civilization profoundly conditioned their lives and, I believe, stimulated their imaginations, freed them from instinctive respect for traditional establishments, and encouraged them to create a new political world. The results of their efforts—however groping, unfinished, and tentative—proved to be a turning point in the political history of Western civilization, radiating out through Europe and Latin America with effects that were as important as they are difficult to interpret.

Through all the chapters two themes, two convictions, remain constant: that these were truly creative people, and that their creative efforts, the generation-long enterprise that elevated these obscure people from their marginal world to the center of Western civilization, were full of inconsistencies, logical dilemmas, and unresolved problems. I have attempted to explain the ambiguities that so beset Jefferson's career; the strange interplay between lofty idealism and cunning realism in Franklin's spectacular success in Paris (and along the way the interplay between that high-spirited, suave, humorous, insouciant *philosophe* and his dutiful, upright, earnest, worried, neo-Puritan colleague Adams). I have similarly sought to explore the desperate struggle of the writers of the *Federalist* papers to reconcile the need for a powerful, coercive public authority with the preservation of the private liberties for which the Revolution had been fought, and, in a wider perspective, to sketch the reception, itself ambiguous, of the Founders' tensely balanced thought by political reformers throughout the Atlantic world.

The Founders were remarkably articulate people. They wrote easily, profusely, and clearly, and they left to posterity a monumental record of their thoughts, their struggles, and their accomplishments. But sometimes words, however profuse and precise, fail: they are so embedded in unconscious assumptions and unquestioned, unperceived conditions that they leave unremarked essentials of people's lives. Images—visual representations—can sometimes illuminate these elusive elements. And so I have used images—to gauge the dimensions of the Founders' provincialism, the subtlety of Franklin's artful self-imaging, and the peculiar idealization of America's revolution abroad in what has been called the age of the democratic revolution.

What follows, therefore, are sketches, assessments of essential elements in a complex history. If these probes convey a sense of the accomplishments of this extraordinary generation together with an awareness of the ambiguities, uncertainties, and perplexities in what they did—difficulties that persist into our own time—they will serve a useful purpose.

B.B.

# I

## Politics and the Creative Imagination

For some time I have been puzzling over the sources of the creative imagination. I began close to home with an effort some years ago to probe the creative imagination among historians,[1] but I have tried to go beyond that, to uncover some general clues to the sources of those mysterious impulses that propel the mind beyond familiar ground into unexpected territories—that account for the sudden appearance of creative configurations of thought, expression, vision, or sound.

At times the creative imagination seems to work in isolation, when an individual, impelled by some uninstructed spark of originality, glimpses relationships or possibilities never seen before, or devises forms of expression never heard before. But most often the creative imagination does not flare in isolation. Creative minds stimulate each other, interaction and competition have a generative effect, sparks fly from disagreement and rivalry, and entire groups become creative. We know something about how that has happened—how such creative groups have formed—in art, in science, in scholarship, and in literature; but the same, I believe, has happened in politics, though in ways we do not commonly perceive. I do not mean sudden turns in legislation or public policy. I mean the recasting of the world of power, the re-formation of the structure of public authority, of the accepted forms of governance, obedience, and resistance, in practice as well as in theory.

The creative reorganization of the world of power and all its implications has happened at various points in history, but rarely, if ever, I believe, as quickly, as successfully, and—so it seems to me—as mysteriously as by a single generation on the eastern shores of North America two hundred years ago.

The Founders of the American nation were one of the most creative groups in modern history. Some among them, especially in recent years, have been condemned for their failures and weaknesses—for their racism, sexism, compromises, and violations of principle. And indeed moral judgments are as necessary in assessing the lives of these people as of any others. But we are privileged to know and to benefit from the outcome of their efforts, which they could only hopefully imagine, and ignore their main concern: which was the possibility, indeed the probability, that their creative enterprise—not to recast the social order but to transform the political system—would fail: would collapse into chaos or autocracy. Again and again they were warned of the folly of defying the received traditions, the sheer unlikelihood that they, obscure people on the outer borderlands of European civilization, knew better than the established authorities that ruled them; that they could successfully create something freer, ultimately more enduring than what was then known in the centers of metropolitan life.

Since we inherit and build on their achievements, we now know what the established world of the eighteenth century flatly denied but which they broke through convention to propose—that absolute power need not be indivisible but can be shared among states within a state and among branches of government, and that the sharing of power and the balancing of forces can create not anarchy but freedom.

We know for certain what they could only experimentally and prayerfully propose—that formal, written constitutions, upheld by judicial bodies, can effectively constrain the tyrannies of both executive force and populist majorities.

We know, because they had the imagination to perceive it, that there is a sense, mysterious as it may be, in which human rights can be seen to exist independent of privileges, gifts, and donations of the powerful, and that these rights can somehow be defined and protected by the force of law.

We casually assume, because they were somehow able to imagine, that the exercise of power is no natural birthright but must be a gift of those who are subject to it.

And we know, what Jefferson so imaginatively perceived and brilliantly expressed, that religion—religion of any kind—in the hands of power can be the worst kind of tyranny—that, as he wrote in his most eloquent state paper,

> to suffer the civil magistrate to intrude his powers into the field of opinion and to restrain the profession or propagation of principles on [the] supposition of their ill tendency is a dangerous fallacy . . . because [the magistrate] being, of course, judge of that tendency will make his opinions the rule of judgment . . . Truth [Jefferson concluded in his Act for Establishing Religious Freedom] is great and will prevail if left to herself . . . she is the proper and sufficient antagonist to error, and has nothing to fear from the conflict unless, by human interposition, disarmed of her natural weapons, free argument and debate—errors ceasing to be dangerous when it is permitted freely to contradict them.[2]

These were extraordinary flights of creative imagination—political heresies at the time, utopian fantasies—and their authors and sponsors knew that their efforts to realize these aspirations had no certain outcomes. Nothing was assured; the future was unpredictable. Everywhere there were turns and twists that had not been expected. Though they searched the histories they knew, consulted the learned authorities of the day, and reviewed the masterworks of political theory, they found few precedents to follow, no models to imitate. They struggled with logical, ideological, and conceptual problems that seemed to have no solutions. The deeper they went the more difficult the problems appeared.

So they were asked: How could constitutions that were to restrict the exercise of power effectively dominate the agencies that had created them?

Were individual rights to be protected against the state? Who could define them?

Conscience was declared to be free. But was not religion, and specifically Christianity, the ultimate source of morality and probity and hence of justice and fairness? So should Christianity not be enforced as a matter of state policy?

There was no end to the problems, and there was never any certainty in the outcome. Some of the problems in the course of time would be solved, some persist to this day and will never be fully resolved. But what strikes one most forcefully in surveying the struggles and achievements of that distant generation is less what they failed to do than what they did do, and the problems that they did in fact solve. One comes away from encounters with that generation, not with a sense of their failings and hypocrisies—they were imperfect people, bound by the limitations of their own world—but with a sense of how alive with creative imaginings they were; how bold they were in transcending the world they had been born into.

How did that happen? What accounts for their creative imagination? What conditions made it possible?

I do not know the answers to those questions. But surveying that lost, remote world, one comes repeatedly on a distinctive element that seems to have played a significant role. It does not account for individual genius, for the sheer power of intellection or for the inspired capacity to reconfigure familiar elements into new patterns and structures. These are the ultimate qualities of the creative imagination. Yet there are circumstances, underlying conditions, that have an empowering force on latent capacities that otherwise would remain inert.


In a brief but brilliant essay entitled "Provincialism," the art critic Kenneth Clark commented on the differences between metropolitan and provincial art. Through the centuries, he wrote, metropolitan art, emerging from dominant centers of culture, has set the grand styles that have radiated out into the world, creating standards and forming assumptions that only idiots, Clark wrote, would challenge. But in time metropolitan art, for all its successes—and in part because of them—becomes repetitive, overrefined, academic, self-absorbed as it elaborates, polishes, and attenuates its initial accomplishments. A kind of scholasticism sets in, while out on the margins, removed from the metropolitan centers, provincial art develops free of those excesses. Artists on the periphery introduce simplicity and common sense to a style that has become too embellished, too sophisticated, too self-centered. The provincials are concrete in their visualization, committed to the ordinary facts of life as they know them rather than to an established style that has taken on a life of its own. And they have a visionary intensity, which at times attains a lyrical quality, as they celebrate the world around them and strive to realize their fresh ambitions.

There are dangers in the provincial arts, Clark points out: insularity; regression into primitivism; complacence in the comforting familiarity of local scenes. But the most skillful provincial artists have the vigor of fresh energies; they are immersed in and stimulated by the ordinary reality around them; and they transcend their limited environments by the sheer intensity of their vision, which becomes, at the height of their powers, prophetic.[3]

Thus Kenneth Clark on provincialism in art. To a remarkable degree I believe the same might be said of provincialism in politics and the political imagination—particularly the politics of Revolutionary America.

The American founders were provincials—living on the outer borderlands of an Atlantic civilization whose heartlands were the metropolitan centers of England, France, the Netherlands, and Spain. The world they were born into was so deeply provincial, so derivative in its culture, that it is difficult for us now to imagine it as it really was—difficult for us to reorient our minds to that small, remote world. We cannot avoid reading back our powerful cosmopolitan present, the sense we have of our global authority and our expanded social consciences—reading back all of that into that small, unsure, preindustrial borderland world. Language can mislead us. The vocabulary of politics in eighteenth-century America was metropolitan, transcultural, European if not universal; but the reality of the Americans' lives, the political and social context in North America, was parochial, and the provincialism of those borderland people had, I believe, in political thought precisely those creative qualities that Clark describes in provincial art.

How provincial were they? There is literary evidence, some of it eloquent. William Byrd II, returning to Virginia in 1726 after ten years of intense striving in England's literary and political circles, called his native land a "silent country," in which at times he felt he was "being buried alive." Though surrounded by "my flocks and my herds," he wrote back to England, "my bond-men and bond-women, and every soart of trade amongst my own servants," he was lonely. There was no one to respond to his wit, his satire; no one to acknowledge his intellectual achievements, no way to establish his worth as a man of letters, as a man of the world. He was no longer in the world. Nostalgically, he kept his rooms in London, practiced his languages—every day some Greek and Latin and a bit of Hebrew—read diligently, remorselessly, in several European languages, built up his library into a formidable collection of over three thousand titles, and continued to write, for his own satisfaction, while pouring out to his diary his longings for a greater world.[4]

There were other isolated bookmen and old-fashioned virtuosi—the learned Pennsylvania Quaker James Logan, for example, more successful and consequential a scholar and scientist than Byrd—who were similarly remote from the metropolitan culture, similarly dependent on echoes from abroad. And later, in the pre-Revolutionary years, there would be an outpouring of belles lettres in the North American towns and cities—a plethora of literary efforts and polite discourses in coffeehouses, clubs, salons, and tea tables, all "aping metropolitan rites and fashions," all aspiring to images of a greater beau monde, all refracting metropolitan styles in amusement, wit, and social discourse.

So Thomas Dale, a well-educated London physician down on his luck, emigrated to Charleston, South Carolina, rose through his professional skills and his reputation as what he called "a great wit and a great Scholard," a veritable "vir literatus," to achieve, in that center of provincial culture, wealth, position, and status, while pumping his English correspondents for word of literary developments in London, inquiring after his old acquaintances and literary idols, and hoping that his friends, in their "walks thro' Moorfields and the Stalls . . . would pick me up some pamphlets and 2 or 3 penniworth of Learning good and old." He would consider that "a singular favour,"

> *For Fortune plac'd me in a ruder soil,*
> *Far from the Joys that with my Soul agree,*
> *From wit, from Learning—far, oh far from thee!*[5]

Later, in 1763, Benjamin Franklin, back in urban and enterprising Philadelphia after years in England, knew better than anyone else how far that city had advanced in literary accomplishments in the years since he had launched his Junto's program of cultural development. But he wondered why it was that the "petty island" from which he had just returned—a mere stepping-stone in a brook next to America, "scarce enough of it above water to keep one's shoes dry"—should have, in almost every neighborhood, more sensible, virtuous, and elegant minds than could be collected in "100 leagues of our vast forests." The most gifted Americans, he wrote, merely "lisp attempts at painting, poetry, and musick."[6]

But the witness of art and architecture is more objective and more revealing.

The young John Adams spoke with envy of the rich and powerful in his world, of a smug, arrogant American aristocracy, of elegant American mansions, of grand estates and grand prospects.[7] But what was the scale? How grand was grand?

Some of the grand places he and his contemporaries knew are familiar to us—they have survived or been rebuilt—though we do not often think of them in this connection:

* Longfellow House, in Cambridge, Massachusetts (1759) [fig. 1]
* The Wentworth-Gardner House, in Portsmouth, New Hampshire (1760), built with wealth derived from timber contracts with the British navy [fig. 2]
* Westover, the Byrds' famous house in Virginia (1730–34) [figs. 3, 4]

Fig. 1: Longfellow House

Fig. 2: Wentworth-Gardner House

Fig. 3: Westover—view from the river

Fig. 4: Westover—side view

* Carter's Grove (1750–53), with its handsome entrance hall [figs. 5, 6]
* George Mason's Gunston Hall (1755–58), the "Palladian Room" [figs. 7, 8]
* Van Cortlandt Manor (1740s), on the Hudson, forty miles from Manhattan, built with third-generation Anglo-Dutch wealth [fig. 9].

These are typical houses of the American aristocracy that Adams knew. But how shall we understand their scale? How grand were they? With what should they be compared? What is the range of possibilities?

Fig. 5: Carter's Grove—exterior

Fig. 6: Carter's Grove—entrance hall

Fig. 7: Gunston Hall

Fig. 8: Gunston Hall—Palladian Room

Fig. 9: Van Cortlandt Manor

There is no possible correspondence, no remote connection, between these provincial dwellings and the magnificent showplaces of the English nobility—those vast domestic palaces,

> ornate and massive, with their pedimented porticoes, their spreading balustraded wings—their colonnaded entrance halls, whence the Adam staircase sweeps up beneath a fluted dome; their cream and gilt libraries piled with sumptuous editions of the classics; their orangeries peopled with casts from the antique—all combine to produce an extraordinary impression of culture and elegance and established power.[8]

Marlborough's Blenheim, the Devonshires' Chatsworth, the Marquesses of Bath's Longleat, Walpole's Houghton [figs. 10–14] are in a different world, remote and irrelevant.

Fig. 10:  Blenheim Palace

Fig. 11:  Chatsworth

Fig. 12: Longleat

Fig. 13: Houghton

Fig. 14: Houghton—drawing room

Incomparable too are the sprawling dwellings of long-established English families that had grown organically bit by bit and year by year as successive generations had added extensions and ornaments until what had begun as medieval manor houses became eighteenth-century mansions—"patchwork houses," they have been called, but imposing and handsome. The Sidney family's Penshurst had grown that way, to attain, in Sir Philip Sidney's day, "a firm stateliness," its "exceeding lastingness made the eye believe it was exceedingly beautiful."[9]

Between Chatsworth in Derbyshire and Westover in Virginia—between Longleat and Carter's Grove—the scales are incommensurate. Yet there are meaningful comparisons, especially with the properties of the English gentry in Britain's domestic borderlands—more remote places, like William Weddell's Newby Hall in northeast Yorkshire. Weddell and Newby Hall, in fact, have a peculiar place in North American history since in order to finance his building plans Weddell raised his rents, with the result that a veritable village of his tenants left the land and emigrated across the Atlantic, where their destinies have been traced.[10]

Fig. 15: Newby Hall

Fig. 16: Newby Hall—entrance hall

Fig. 17: Newby Hall—staircase

Fig. 18: Newby Hall—Tapestry Room

In its exterior appearance [fig. 15] Newby Hall is not of a different scale from Byrd's Westover, but once within the house one begins to see the differences. The entrance hall [fig. 16], with its marbled floor, is spacious, its furnishings, which include a handsome chamber

Fig. 19: Newby Hall—
Statue Gallery

Fig. 20:
Newby Hall—Statue
Gallery, detail

organ, solid and elegantly constructed. The staircase [fig. 17] is broad and graceful, and the Tapestry Room [fig. 18] is different from anything in North America: the Palladian Room of George Mason's Gunston Hall is a small country parlor in comparison. The hangings in the Tapestry Room were made on order by the Gobelin factory to designs by Boucher; and the chairs were designed and made by Chippendale. But Weddell's pride and joy—"the admiration of all connoisseurs," a contemporary wrote—was his specially constructed Statue Gallery [fig. 19]. Three linked porticoed spaces, it was cunningly designed by Robert Adam to exhibit the contents of nineteen chests of statuary that Weddell had shipped from Rome in the same months of 1765 when the Americans, on the far periphery of his world, were rebelling against the Stamp Act duties. Dramatically placed at the end of the third space were, and still are, his two main treasures, the wonderful Venus, once in the Palazzo Barberini in Rome, for which Weddell paid a great sum—some said £3,500, some £6,000—and the statue of Athene, for which he paid over £1,000 [fig. 20].[11]

There is nothing in the American world to compare with this. Weddell too was a provincial Briton, though affluent and well connected. His imposing establishment was built in the midst of rural Yorkshire. Even today the contrast between the small sculpture gallery and its surroundings "comes as a shock. It has the force of revelation." What distinguishes him from his affluent American counterparts was not his wealth—the estate of the Virginian Robert "King" Carter, at his death in 1732, was reported to include 300,000 acres, 1,000 slaves, and £10,000 in cash; and mercantile fortunes in pre-Revolutionary Philadelphia could reach £80,000.[12] What distinguishes Weddell was his cultural awareness, the worldliness of his sensibilities—in a word, his sophistication.


And what of the people, the American aristocracy, the local elite— what of their style, their manner, the images they projected? We know how they presented themselves: many portraits survive. Sometimes

Fig. 21: Jeremiah Lee                    Fig. 22: Mrs. Jeremiah Lee

they posed theatrically, self-consciously, with somewhat painfully contrived elegance heightened by the painters'—especially Copley's—
ambitions. They are substantial, proud, aspiring people, like

* the stolid Jeremiah Lee of Marblehead, Massachusetts, and his
  equally stolid, somewhat jowly wife, carrying, as she cautiously
  ascends the stairs, a bunch of fruit, symbol of fertility, in the lap of
  her voluminous gown [figs. 21, 22],
* Isaac Smith of New York, and the formidable, matronly, no-
  nonsense Mrs. Smith, also nestling fruit in the lap of her dress
  [figs. 23, 24],
* Thomas Mifflin of Philadelphia, a wealthy, well-traveled Quaker,
  later quartermaster general of the American army and governor
  of Pennsylvania, and his beady-eyed wife [fig. 25],

and a succession of Boston's shrewdest, most successful men of
business:

Fig. 23: Isaac Smith

Fig. 24: Mrs. Isaac Smith

Fig. 25: Mr. and Mrs. Thomas Mifflin

Fig. 26: Peter Faneuil

Fig. 27: John Erving

Fig. 28: Eleazer Tyng

* Peter Faneuil [fig. 26],
* John Erving [fig. 27],
* Eleazer Tyng [fig. 28].

With what images should these portraits of the provincial, bourgeois elite be compared? Not of course with such worldly, resplendently portrayed magnificos, utterly remote from America, as

* William, Duke of Cumberland, the victor over the Scots in the rebellion of '45 [fig. 29]; or
* the flamboyant, infamous Georgiana, Duchess of Devonshire [fig. 30].

Fig. 30: Georgiana, Duchess of Devonshire

Fig. 29: William, Duke of Cumberland

Fig. 31: Earl of Hillsborough

Fig. 32: Mary, Countess Howe

Nor is the comparison very useful even with the less grand, less Olympian aristocracy who did have direct connections with America:

* the Earl of Hillsborough, for example, whose imperious attitude toward America when he was secretary of state and whose personal snubs Benjamin Franklin never forgot and never forgave [fig. 31]; or
* the graceful, elegant, confident Mary, Countess Howe [fig. 32], whose husband, Sir Richard, would lead the naval forces against America in the Revolution.

The most meaningful comparisons must be with the humbler domestic gentry, people like Gainsborough's immediate neighbors and friends in the Suffolk countryside, near his native village of Sudbury, whom he immortalized in stylized, leisured, witty poses against the background of their property:

* Mr. and Mrs. Andrews—young newlyweds, somewhat supercilious, elegantly clothed, he crosslegged, informal, with gun and

Fig. 33: Mr. and Mrs. Andrews

Fig. 34: Mr. and Mrs. William Hallett

Fig. 35: John Plampin

dog, she "sitting pertly in her best blue satin dress, the folds of which are loosely and exquisitely modelled"; they face but are not involved in their gleaming, fecund fields [fig. 33],[13]

* Mr. and Mrs. William Hallett, a near-caricature of studied, moody, romantic nonchalance [fig. 34], and
* the roguishly relaxed squire John Plampin, no less stylish and fashionable for all the seeming abandon of his pose [fig. 35].

Again, there is a different level of worldliness and sophistication—not so much a matter of wealth, but of style, and the sense, even if contrived, of what Edmund Burke called the necessary condition of any true aristocracy: uncontending ease, the unbought grace of life.

Two American portraits illustrate the contrasts more precisely. Two leaders of the Revolutionary generation who played key roles in the creative restructuring of public law and institutions came, as it happened, from Connecticut. Both were painted by Ralph Earl when they were at the height of their powers; and Earl—less fashionable, less polished a painter than Copley, less dramatic, less artistically ambitious, his work less stylized, more flatly descriptive—was closer to the grain of reality. He captured something of the essential qualities of these provincial public men and something elemental in their culture.

The first is a portrait of Oliver Ellsworth and his wife.

Ellsworth—a lawyer, jurist, and politician; a key figure in the Philadelphia convention; one of the first to formulate the principle of judicial review of legislation, hence the juridical enforcement of a written constitution. As a senator, he drafted the great Judiciary Act of 1789, which created the federal court system, and he devised the first set of Senate rules and the legislative procedures for admitting new states, something unheard of in European public law. Thereafter he served as Chief Justice of the Supreme Court and commissioner to France.

Like the Halletts and Andrewses, Ellsworth and his wife present themselves as a prosperous couple against the background of their property: in the Ellsworths' case, their renovated "seat," as it was called, in Windsor, Connecticut [fig. 36; see also color insert]. But the contrast of this proud, stiff, carefully dressed provincial couple with

Fig. 36:  Mr. and Mrs. Oliver Ellsworth

the Halletts and Andrewses could not be more vivid. There is no studied casualness here, nothing leisured or witty in the pose. The Ellsworths sit rigidly alert, their posture and appurtenances unsophisticated, old-fashioned. Mrs. Ellsworth, then only thirty-six but the mother of nine children, has on a silk robe over a matching silk skirt; she wears a stiff muslin collar and that strange, starched head-dress typical of provincial gentlewomen of the time. And Ellsworth seems almost didactic as he sits displaying a copy of the Constitution. His expression is arresting. Earl caught the man's intelligence and firmness, his essential gravitas, lightened, though, by a very slight suggestion of good humor [fig. 37]. There is about this forth-right, self-confident, unaffected man an understated, quiet dignity and the simplicity that made him a popular figure in his native Connecticut village even at the height of his national and international fame. And behind the couple are their fields and house [fig. 38]. The landscape is plain, unadorned, unromanticized—no gleaming acres of idealized golden wheat, but a few elm trees and a bare, spacious yard divided by fences of palings behind which, on a slight rise, is their clapboard two-storey house.[14]

Figs. 37, 38: Mr. and Mrs. Oliver Ellsworth, details

Fig. 39: Roger Sherman

Even more revealing is Earl's portrait of Roger Sherman, the self-educated farmer, shoemaker, surveyor, lawyer, jurist, merchant, and landowner; a member of the committees that drafted the Declaration of Independence and the Articles of Confederation; chairman of the committee at the Philadelphia convention whose "Connecticut Com-

Fig. 40: Roger Sherman—Statuary Hall

promise" created the bicameral structure of the United States Congress; Federalist pamphleteer in the ratification struggle; controversial figure in devising the Bill of Rights; and United States senator. He was, John Adams said, as "honest as an angel and as firm in the cause of American Independence as Mount Atlas." Sherman did not "pose" for Earl—he was incapable of "posing" for anyone. He quite literally "sat" for him, and the result is one of the most striking portraits of the age [fig. 39; see also color insert].[15]

Sherman is utterly unpretentious and unselfconscious. The painting is honest down to the worn spot on the right knee; he is wigless and sternly, starkly unfashionable. Later, in the nineteenth century his image would be wonderfully transformed into that of a Roman statesman suitable for the Capitol's Statuary Hall [fig. 40]. But Earl's portrait tells the truth. Sherman was rustic, clumsy in manner, terse, a severely self-disciplined and unbending Calvinist, close to the soil and to small-scale mechanical arts. Yet, though the ultimate American provincial, he was one of the most innovative political thinkers of his age. He was awkward, a contemporary wrote, and "unaccountably strange in his manner"—"the oddity of his address, the vulgarisms that accompany his public speaking . . . make everything that is connected with him grotesque and laughable." Yet, despite all of that, "in his train of thinking there is something regular, deep and comprehensive."[16]

Earl's stiffly posed, resolute faces—and even Copley's glossier and more fashionable portrayals of American businessmen, lawyers, and politicians—reflect the consciousness of recently earned distinctions and relatively shallow prosperity. If these people formed an aristocracy it was not a very secure, graceful, or elevated aristocracy. Their acquisitions were within the reach of everyday competition; they lacked the magnificence by which a ruling order in the eighteenth century reinforced itself. Striving, searching, and tense, they were, and were aware of being, provincials.

But what of such worldly figures as Jefferson and Franklin? Jefferson was the friend, indeed confidant, of Condorcet, Lafayette, and La Rochefoucauld; advisor to the liberal noblemen who began the French Revolution; correspondent of Scottish philosophers and English scientists alike. Was he not the ultimate cosmopolitan in his deep appreciation of European art, architecture, technology, philosophy, science, and history? But it was he who wrote so famously from Paris that "no American should come to Europe under thirty years of age." For in Europe, he warned, an American acquires a fondness for luxury and dissipation and a contempt for the simplicity of his own country, gets entangled in "female intrigue destructive of his own and others' happiness, or a passion for whores destructive of his health, and in both cases learns to consider fidelity to the marriage bed as an ungentlemanly practice and inconsistent with happiness." Jefferson was, in fact—despite the breadth of his learning and his likely relationship with a slave woman—a provincial puritan. He lectured his daughter Patsy, studying at a fashionable French convent, on the importance of "the needle and domestic economy" in the simple society to which they would return, and he longed to be back in Monticello.[17]

Franklin, of course, floated easily in French salon society, but, keenly aware of his provincial origin, he shrewdly overcame its stigma in France by flaunting it—cleverly establishing his cosmopolitan credentials by exaggerating, caricaturing, hence implicitly denying, his provincialism. He knew that by projecting himself as a gifted backwoods innocent, he would become nature's own scientist and philosopher, and thus the very embodiment of the fashionable ideas of the *philosophes* [chap. 3, fig. 44].

The Founders were provincials, alive to the values of a greater world, but not, they knew, of it—comfortable in a lesser world but aware of its limitations.

And as provincials, in the pre-Revolutionary years, their view of the world was discontinuous. Two forces, two magnets, affected their efforts to find standards and styles: the values associated with unaffected native simplicity and those to be found in an acquired cosmopolitan sophistication. For many—the ablest, best informed, and most ambitious—the result was a degree of rootlessness, of alienation either from the higher sources of culture or from the familiar local environment. Few whose perceptions surpassed local boundaries—and over one thousand Americans traveled to Europe in the generation before the Revolution[18]—could rest content with a simple, consistent image of themselves. Their view of the world and of their place in it was ambivalent, uncertain; and that ambivalence tended to shake their minds from the roots of habit and tradition. Like the eighteenth-century Scots, whose similar borderland situation stimulated an extraordinary renaissance in letters, natural science, and social science, the Americans' ambivalent identities led them to the interstices of metropolitan thought where were found new views and new approaches to the old.[19]

Never having been fully immersed in, never fully committed to or comfortable with, the cosmopolitan establishment, in the crucible of the Revolution they challenged its authority, and when faced with the great problems of public life they turned to their own local, provincial experiences for solutions. Like Clark's provincial artists, they adhered to the facts of everyday life, and from them developed a fresh vision of what might be accomplished, what might be created. "The 'axioms' of Montesquieu or any other great man," the New Jersey lawyer, engineer, and political pamphleteer John Stevens wrote, "tho' [others] shall deem them 'as irrefragable as any in Euclid,' shall never persuade me to quarrel with my bread and butter." "Is it not the glory of the people of America," Madison wrote,

> that whilst they have paid a decent regard to the opinions of former times and other nations, they have not suffered a blind veneration for antiquity, for custom, or for names to overrule the suggestions of their own good sense, the knowledge of their own situation, and the lessons of their own experience?[20]

So they referred the great, classic problems of politics not to the experience of the ages or to the wisdom of the metropolitan authorities, but to their own provincial situation, and developed their ideas and their vision of the future from what they knew to be true, and then shaped them to conform to the idealistic programs of political reform that were elsewhere deemed hopelessly utopian.

They attacked head-on the overrefined, overelaborated, dogmatic metropolitan formulas in political thought, challenging assumptions that only idiots, they were indeed told, would question.

So the great men had said, and the metropolitan world demonstrated, that dual sovereignties—sovereign states within a sovereign state—could not coexist. That would lead, it had forever been said, systematically and inevitably, to conflict and chaos, for sovereign power was in its nature indivisible. But "I ask," Ellsworth declared in a pivotal moment in the ratification debate, "*why* can they not [coexist]? It is not enough to *say* they cannot. I wish for some reason . . . It is vain to say, they cannot [co]exist, when they actually have done it."[21] Their constitutional solution to this ancient problem—federalism: imperfect but effective—was a formalization of the de facto constitutional world that they, as British provincials ruled by both their local assemblies and Parliament, had known for generations.

So they reconsidered the immemorial doctrine of the separation of powers, and recast the elements involved from legalized social orders—crown, nobility, and commons—which had never been a direct part of their lives, to functioning branches of government—executive, legislative, judicial—which had been.

So too they confronted the authorities—Montesquieu above all—who propounded as dogma the idea that free republican states, like the Swiss cantons, must be small. Knowledgeable people had said again and again that large republics, ruled by the people themselves and lacking the coercive power of monarchies, would simply splinter and crumble into anarchy until order was restored by military force. How could representative government and consensual law reach into the raw outer fringes of an extended republic?

To this they replied that the form of representation that had developed naturally in the remote American provinces simply demolished such received logic. The actual representation of interests and people in the governments of these colonies—as opposed to Europe's representation of estates and privileged localities—made the extension of the nation to continental proportions perfectly compatible with republican freedoms. Ancient and modern thinkers both, they said, simply had no notion, because they had no experience, of the dynamic system of representation that had grown up in America—a system that shifted with the growth and movement of the population and in which representatives were bound to constituents' wishes. How could Montesquieu, whose ideas had been formed in the Old World, have known of this dynamic system? "Had he been an American," Stevens wrote, "and now living, I would stake my life on it, he would have formed different principles." "For the American states," James Wilson declared in a major address to Pennsylvania's ratifying convention, "were reserved the glory and the happiness of diffusing this vital principle throughout the constituent parts of government."[22]

Disposed, in the upheaval of the Revolution, to find in their own diminished provincial world not deprivation but the source of new advantages—discovering that the glass was half full, not half empty—they weeded out anachronisms in the received tradition, discarded elements that were irrelevant to their provincial situation, and with imagination and an intense vision of what the future might be, built a new structure on the actualities of the provincial world they had known.

But the effect of their provincialism ran deeper than that. As their identity as a separate people took form through the Revolutionary years they came to see that their remoteness from the metropolitan world gave them a moral advantage in politics. The leadership of Britain, like that of the rest of Europe, they learned from innumerable publications and from the hundreds of friends and relatives who returned from visits to the home country, had succumbed to corruption and corrosive cynicism. Since freedom in the end depends on the integrity and to some degree the virtue of rulers and ruled alike, Britain was no longer the bastion of liberty it once had been. America—in the simplicity of its manners, its lack of luxury and pomp, its artlessness, homeliness, lack of affectation and cynicism—America had taken Britain's place as the moral guardian and promoter of liberty. They had no illusions about the innate corruptibility and venality of all people everywhere: "If men were angels," Madison wrote, "no government would be necessary." But they believed that their provincial isolation and lack of great wealth and sources of great power had protected them from the worst dangers of corruption. And so they could live by what Madison called "this great republican principle":

> that the people will have virtue and intelligence to select men of virtue and wisdom. Is there no virtue among us?—If there be not, we are in a wretched situation. No theoretical checks—no form of Government, can render us secure.[23]

In a morally enervated world overcome with corruption, America, they believed, was unique; and their sense of moral integrity, nourished in the awareness of provincial simplicity and innocence and discussed endlessly, almost obsessively, in their political writings, fortified and justified their determination to defy tradition, to build their own, different political world, and to create a new and permanent model for the benevolent use of power.

It was an intensely creative moment in Western history. Great authorities, established theories, the world of metropolitan sophistication were left behind in favor of fresh thought and the wisdom of local experience. Faithful to their provincial lives, convinced of the rightness of the principles they wished to make real, the Revolutionary leaders, Madison wrote, "accomplished a revolution which has no parallel in the annals of human society: They reared the fabrics of governments which have no model on the face of the globe."[24]

Their provincialism, and the sense they derived from it of their own moral stature, had nourished their political imaginations. Uncertain of their place in the established, metropolitan world, they did not think themselves bound by it; they were prepared to challenge it, and, as Thomas Paine put it, to begin the world anew. With fresh energy, and ambitious to recast the overrefined, overly elaborated, canonical system of thought and institutions that had dominated their lives, they sought to achieve a profound transformation of government and politics. Their unlikely experiment on the outer fringes of European civilization threatened the stability of state systems throughout the greater world, and it contained within it a force that would radiate out, however erratically, into areas of social life they had not intended to reform.

In the most general sense, what conditioned and stimulated the Founders' imagination and hence their capacity to begin the world anew was the fact that they came from outside the metropolitan establishment, with all its age-old, deeply buried, arcane entanglements and commitments. From their distant vantage point they viewed what they could see of the dominant order with a cool, critical, challenging eye, and what they saw was something atrophied, weighted down by its own complacent, self-indulgent elaboration, and vulnerable to the force of fresh energies and imaginative designs. Refusing to be intimidated by the received traditions and confident of their own integrity and creative capacities, they demanded to know why things must be the way they are; and they had the imagination and energy to conceive of something closer to the grain of everyday reality and more likely to lead to human happiness.

We have neither their need nor their opportunity to begin the world anew. But we do have the obligation, as inheritors of their success, to view every establishment critically, to remain in some sense on the margins, and forever to ask, with Ellsworth, why things must be the way they are, knowing, as he did, that it is never enough to *say* they must be so—one needs to know *why*.

# II

# Jefferson and the
# Ambiguities of Freedom

The reputations of those who shape the fate of nations become historical forces in themselves. They are twisted and turned to fit the needs of those who follow, until, it seems, there is no actual person left, only a complex mirror in which successive interests see aspects of themselves. Of Jefferson this is doubly—trebly—true. His reputation has had what has been called a "kaleidoscopic changeability." For a century and a half it has been more fluid, more malleable than the reputation of any of the other great figures of the Revolutionary generation, or indeed of anyone else in American history.

The 450 crowded pages of Merrill Peterson's *The Jefferson Image in the American Mind* show the fabulous complexity of the problem that faces those who wish to understand Jefferson and assess fairly his place in American history. Which Jefferson? The Jefferson image, Peterson writes, has been "an ill-arranged cluster of meanings, rancorous, mercurial, fertile . . . [It] was constantly evolving." Endless "errors and legends and myths" have found their way into history—and not, it seems, accidentally. The "hysteria of denunciation and the hysteria of exaltation" that have followed him through the ages were there at the start—in his own lifetime.[1]

Many of his contemporaries idolized him, but others—many others—vilified him. Three generations of Adamses spoke of him venomously. John Adams, his lifelong friend and political opponent, in many ways venerated him, but he disagreed with him on basic principles, and declared at one point that Jefferson was as ambitious as Oliver Cromwell and so "warped by prejudice and so blinded by ignorance as to be unfit for the office he holds . . . As a politician he is a child and the dupe of party!" John Quincy Adams improved on his father's judgment. He conceded that Jefferson had an "ardent passion for liberty and the rights of man" but denounced him for infidelity, "pliability of principle," and double dealing. And *that* Adams's grandson Henry discounted Jefferson's duplicity, but wrote at length, in his monumental history of the Jefferson and Madison administrations, about what he took to be Jefferson's failure as a statesman, his opportunistic abandonment of principles, his willingness to "risk the fate of mankind" to justify his theories, and his fatal incapacity—so caught up was he, Adams said, in delusive visions of the present as a golden age—to recognize that he lived "in a world torn by wars and convulsions and drowned in blood." But it was Hamilton who was Jefferson's chief enemy in politics, and his feelings were never in doubt. Hamilton feared what he called the Virginian's fanaticism and believed he was "crafty" and a "contemptible hypocrite." He worked feverishly for Jefferson's election to the presidency when the contest deadlocked in the House, in part because he was convinced that the alternative, Aaron Burr, would be even worse, and in part because he believed that such was Jefferson's hypocrisy, he was unlikely ever "to do anything in pursuance of his principles which will contravene his popularity, or his interest."[2]

After two hundred years, while the panegyrics continue and Jefferson still stands tall in the pantheon of the Enlightenment, the savagery of condemnation, increasingly embittered by the charge of racism compounded by the likelihood of his sexual relation with his slave Sally Hemings, exceeds anything seen before. Leonard Levy, reviewing Jefferson's record on civil liberties, subtitled his remorseless case for the prosecution (1963) *The Darker Side* ("Jefferson never once risked career or reputation to champion free speech, fair trial, or any other libertarian value . . . The certainty that he was right, combined with his terrifying idealism, led him to risk the fate of the nation"). Michael Zuckerman (1989) declared him to be "a man intellectually undone by his negrophobia . . . he was ultimately prepared to abandon all else in which he believed—and believed passionately—sooner than surrender his racial repugnances." Michael Lind (1995) called Jefferson "in many ways the greatest southern reactionary" whose tradition's "final miserable estuary" lies in the careers of Theodore Bilbo and Strom Thurmond. "Every major feature of the modern United States . . . represents a repudiation of Jeffersonianism." Pauline Maier (1997) argued that "what generations of Americans came to revere [as the Declaration of Independence] was not Jefferson's but Congress's Declaration, the work not of a single man, or even of a committee, but of a larger body of men with the good sense to recognize a 'pretty good' draft [Jefferson's] when they saw it, and who were able to identify and eliminate Jefferson's more outlandish assertions and unnecessary words." Joseph Ellis (1997), while conceding that almost alone among the founding generation Jefferson sought "prescriptions for government that at best protected individual rights and at worst minimized the impact of government . . . on individual lives," concludes that "modern day invocations of Jefferson as the 'apostle of freedom' are invariably misleading and problematic." But it was in Conor Cruise O'Brien's foray into Jeffersoniana (1996) that the attacks on the Virginian reached their peak—or nadir. "It is difficult to resist the conclusion," O'Brien wrote, "that the twentieth century statesman whom the Thomas Jefferson of January 1793 would have admired most is Pol Pot . . . We cannot even say categorically that Jefferson would have condemned the bombing of the federal building in Oklahoma City and the destruction of its occupants." And in any case, "the Ku Klux Klan was ideologically descended from Thomas Jefferson."[3]

The condemnations, from Hamilton to O'Brien, are intemperate, impassioned, remorseless—peculiarly venomous. Yet Jefferson remains a brilliant star in the firmament of American ideals and aspirations. Why the contradictions? Why the anomalies in his image and his reputation?

To some extent they reflect inconsistencies in Jefferson's policies, behavior, and character, which are striking. He said he sincerely loathed slavery, condemned it as "an abominable crime," a "hideous blot" on civilization which must somehow be eliminated, but he did not free his own slaves (except a few, probably related to him, in his will); and at the end of his life he advocated the expansion of slavery into the southwestern states. Was he not the ultimate libertarian, the passionate defender of freedom of speech, of the press, of religion, of protection against illegal searches and seizures, of the sanctity of habeas corpus? His passion for civil liberties radiates through his most profound state paper, the Act for Establishing Religious Freedom. There is nothing to compare with the elegant, emotive lyricism that lies within the formal cadences of that extraordinary document. One must read it aloud to appreciate the perfection of the rhythms and the immaculate choice of words. But when he came to design the curriculum for the University of Virginia's law school he deliberately omitted books whose political and moral views he disapproved of, and the only professors he proposed were those whose political opinions agreed with his own. In the early Revolutionary years he endorsed loyalty oaths; in suppressing the Burr conspiracy he tolerated lapses in habeas corpus; and in attempting to enforce his ill-fated embargo he ignored the Fourth Amendment and ruled, in certain areas and at certain times, by executive decree and the threat of armed force.[4]

The anomalies and apparent inconsistencies seem endless. He avoided partisan debates in public, but urged others to do the opposite, and he helped support a partisan press. He was a pacifist in principle, but he argued for a retributive war against the piratical Barbary states, on the ground that if America meant to be an effective naval power "can we begin it on a more honourable occasion or with a weaker foe?" He said that a little rebellion against oppressive conditions, every now and then, would be a good thing; "the tree of liberty must be refreshed from time to time with the blood of patriots and tyrants" were his famous words. But when the Haitian people rose against their French masters, he declined, as president, to help them. He was a fervent constitutionalist, indeed a strict and narrow constructionist, especially in fighting the Alien and Sedition Acts in 1798; but five years later, in arranging for the purchase of Louisiana, he deliberately exceeded the bounds of the Constitution. "The less we say about the constitutional difficulties respecting Louisiana," he told Madison, his secretary of state, "the better," and he added that if some political maneuvers were necessary to overcome constitutional impediments, they should be done "sub silentio."[5]

So much about Jefferson seemed to contemporaries, as to many historians, contradictory and incongruous. His appearance surprised those who came to pay their respects to the famous statesman, knowing him to be a learned savant, the friend of major figures of the French Enlightenment. Tall, red-headed, and freckled, dressed in ordinary, rather dowdy clothes (yarn stockings, a British official reported with surprise, "and slippers down at the heels"), he sat casually, "in a lounging manner," perched on one hip. There was nothing, one visitor said, "of that firm collected deportment which I expected would dignify the presence of a secretary or minister."[6] Yet everyone recognized that his conversation was wonderfully informed and often brilliant. And why would it not be? Though he was no orator in public forums, he conversed easily, and he was a fabulous polymath: politician, diplomat, architect, draftsman, connoisseur of painting, anthropologist, bibliophile, classicist, musician, lawyer, educator, oenologist, farm manager, agronomist, theologian (or rather, antitheologian), and amateur of almost every branch of science from astronomy to zoology, with special emphasis on paleontology.

Jefferson slipped easily from role to role. His election to the vice-presidency of the United States coincided with his election to the presidency of the American Philosophical Society, a position he enjoyed far more than he did the nation's vice-presidency and which he proudly and actively held for the next eighteen years. In the midst of the ferocious struggle, in 1801, to settle the tie vote in the Electoral College—a vote, resolved only on the thirty-sixth ballot, that would elevate Jefferson to the presidency, transform the American government, and alter the course of American history—he calmly continued his correspondence with a professor of anatomy about the disposal of some recently discovered fossil bones that bore on disputed points of animal life in North America.[7]

His correspondence was prodigious: the editors of the *Jefferson Papers* have located over nineteen thousand letters written by him. They reflect extraordinary energy, a ceaseless flow of ideas on every conceivable subject, and a restless, tenacious mind, as fertile in formulating abstract ideas as in solving the most ordinary, mundane problems. Printing presses, phosphoric matches, cylinder lamps, and the shapes of plowshares fascinated him; so too did the principles of justice and the logical strengths and weaknesses of the thought of Hobbes, Hume, and Destutt de Tracy. He writes of the soil and of the heavens, and of everything in between: of economics and curtain beds; of political theory and "hydrostatic waistcoats"; of international law and carriage springs; of constitutions and macaroni machines; of poetry and pedometers. Through it all there glows a humane and generous purpose: to improve upon the inheritance; to meliorate the condition of life; to broaden the reach of liberty; and to assist in the pursuit of happiness.

Historians will never fully encompass Jefferson's protean versatility, nor will they completely resolve the paradoxes in his career and the apparent contradictions in his character. But there are a few signposts along the way to help one understand some, at least, of the basic elements in his public persona, and perhaps assess a little more accurately the complexity of his character and achievement.

With his enormous vitality and universal curiosity, he seemed forever young. But he was in fact thirty-three in 1776—almost middle-aged, by eighteenth-century standards—and though Madison was younger by only eight years and Hamilton by twelve, they seemed to belong to a different generation. By the end of 1774, when Madison, only a year from college, took his first, very minor public post, and Hamilton was still an undergraduate, Jefferson was an established, successful lawyer and prosperous planter with five years of experience in the House of Burgesses behind him. They had been extremely busy years in politics. On the day he had first taken his seat in the Burgesses, he had drafted the reply to the governor's speech, and in the years that followed he wrote in quick succession several pieces of legislation, Virginia's resolution to oppose the Boston Port Act, a Declaration of Rights for Virginia's Revolutionary convention, and the learned and inflammatory Instructions to Virginia's delegates to the Continental Congress. Sent to Philadelphia in 1775 as Virginia's delegate to the Continental Congress, he contributed to the drafting of the Association, which in effect set the Revolution in motion, and wrote not only the Declaration of the Causes and Necessity for Taking Up Arms but also America's reply to the British conciliatory proposals. And the next year, a month before drafting the Declaration of Independence, he drew up a complete new constitution for the state of Virginia.

That he was chosen to draft the Declaration is hardly surprising if for no other reason than, as John Adams later recalled, Jefferson was known to have "a happy talent of composition." His writings, Adams said, were handed about and remarked on for their "peculiar felicity of expression."[8] But by then Jefferson had acquired something more important than a reputation for learning and literary skill. From his voracious reading, from his extensive knowledge of law, from his acute attention to the views of his teachers and of his colleagues in politics, and from his instinctive understanding of independence as he had personally experienced it on his borderland plantations, he had developed a comprehensive view of politics, freedom, and America's unique role in world history which would shape all of his thought and much of his actions thereafter.

It was not simply that he had helped to construct the pattern of ideas, beliefs, attitudes, and aspirations that we think of as the ideology of the American Revolution. He had personally *achieved* it— within the limits of the world he knew he had reached it, through years of study, thought, and public controversy. To break through the barriers of the ancien régime and to formulate and act on the principles of freedom was a triumph of enlightened thought which, he hoped, would usher in a new era in human history. In that happy time, which he felt America could now approach, legislatures would be truly representative; popular majorities would rule; the institutions of government would be strictly separated so that no person or group of people would exercise undue power; power itself would be restricted; establishments of religion would be forever banished; and the human freedoms for which mankind had yearned—freedom of speech, of the press, of worship, and the right to the security of property and to impartial judicial proceedings presided over by judges independent of political pressures—all this would be perfectly protected by the instruments of free government.

And beyond the realm of government, Jefferson glimpsed, in these early, formative years, and never lost, a vision of human felicity—a romantic vision, of sensible, hard-working, independent folk secure in their possession of land, free of the corruptions of urban poverty and cynicism, free of dependence on a self-indulgent aristocracy of birth, responsible to the common good as well as to personal better-ment, educated in the essentials of free government and committed to the principles of freedom—peaceful, self-reliant, self-respecting, and unintimidated people. Occasionally the sheer romanticism of this vision would break through. "Ours," he informed Crèvecoeur in 1787, "are the only farmers who can read Homer." He was certain, after a year in France, that of the twenty million people in that coun-try, "nineteen millions [are] more wretched, more accursed in every circumstance of human existence, than the most conspicuously wretched individual of the whole United States." In France, as else-where in Europe,

> conjugal love having no existence among them, domestic happi-ness, of which that is the basis, is utterly unknown . . . [Their pur-suits] offer only moments of extasy [sic] amidst days and months of restlessness and torment. Much, very much inferior this to the tranquil, permanent felicity with which domestic society in Amer-ica blesses most of its inhabitants, leaving them to follow steadily those pursuits which health and reason approve, and rendering truly delicious the intervals of these pursuits.[9]

These visions engrossed his mind and imagination. But he was never confident that these goals could be reached. It would, inevitably, he believed, be a constant struggle, and the outcome would always be in doubt. For along with the ideals of radical reform and the principles of freedom, he had inherited the belief, pervasive in radical thought in Britain for over a century, that freedom was in its nature a fragile plant that had been and would be, again and again, overwhelmed by the forces of power; that where freedom had survived it remained beset by those who lusted for domination. Even in Britain, its last bastion in Europe, Jefferson thought, freedom, overwhelmed by the corruption of Walpole's government early in the century, had finally been destroyed by the autocracy of George III and his junto of ministers, whose depredations Jefferson itemized so fully in the Declaration.[10]

But the evils that had overwhelmed Britain were not unique to those once-heroic people. They arose, Jefferson believed, from human nature itself, and would take whatever form immediate situations might require. And so, though Americans seemed free of the worst evils and had set out on a new path, he knew that the realization of this vision was uncertain at best. Everything would depend on the sheer survival of the Revolutionary nation, and thereafter on its continued adherence to the principles of freedom as he had understood them in the early years of the struggle. Dangers from the inevitable counterforces were certain to appear on all sides, and in new and unexpected forms.

But if Jefferson had been only a radical and eloquent idealist, fearful that the achievement of freedom was precarious at best, forever beset by dangers that could easily overwhelm it, he would never have played the powerful role in history that he did. Coupled—incongruously—with his soaring idealism was the realism and hardheaded pragmatism of an excellent "man of business." Fantastically industrious, administratively efficient, with a true instinct for the moment to act and the moment to relent, Jefferson was a natural politician, as shrewd and calculating as the best and more effective than most.

He tackled the most complex political and economic problems with tireless zest. He was incapable of boredom. In a six-month

period in Paris he finished a detailed consular treaty with the French
government; wrote a technical treatise on the American whale fish-
ery based on data he had been methodically collecting for several
years; drew up a proposal for funding the foreign debt of the United
States; continued a long correspondence on outfitting American ves-
sels in the French fleet; wrote extensively, though surreptitiously, to
Lafayette on how to manage the developing revolution in Paris;
drafted cunning messages to keep the United States government
from being blackmailed; and sent practical advice repeatedly to an
unfortunate Virginian whose family affairs were falling to pieces.[11]

The Paris years were crowded with business efficiently handled,
but his work as ambassador was preparatory to his labors as secretary of state and president. The leading student of his presidency
concludes that "Jefferson brought to the presidency the most system
in administration and the strongest leadership that the office had yet
experienced." He had all the qualities of a successful political executive. He balanced decisiveness with accountability; he relied on discussion and persuasion rather than authority; and he was tolerant of
dissenting views. "The first President to make the Cabinet system
work," he established a close relationship with Congress. And
beyond that, he kept in touch with the population at large, and made
voters more conscious of, and involved in, the political process than
they had ever been before.[12]

All of this was the work of a natural politician and an industrious,
efficient administrator—abilities not normally associated with radical idealism. But in Jefferson that unlikely association existed, and it
is the key, I believe, to the complexities of his public career and to the
strange oscillations of his fame. If he had been less responsive to the
principles of freedom as they had emerged in the initial struggle with
Britain, less committed to the vision of a golden age, and more cautious in seeking it, he might, when in positions of power, have been
less likely to have had to modify or complicate or contradict his principles in attempting, in his efficient way, to effect them, and so in the
end might have seemed more consistent and less likely to be thought
hypocritical.

How different, in this, was he from his two younger contemporaries, who emerged on the scene after independence had been achieved and so inherited the Revolution, and took its principles for granted. Madison, Jefferson's lifelong friend, collaborator, and political ally, was quizzical and skeptical. His mind was less capacious and less elevated than Jefferson's, but more close-grained, original, and instinctively contrary. Less learned than Jefferson, his verbal skills inferior, he was almost pedantically alert to inner complications, and so, though less adept a politician, he was more consistent. Jefferson would, if need be, jump out of a syllogism to save the major premise; Madison, less deductive, did not need such complicated gymnastics. And Hamilton, much younger in years and even younger in spirit, responded to different voices altogether—voices of a social and economic world just emerging, whose relation to Jefferson's ideals could be discordant.

So it was Jefferson—simultaneously a radical utopian idealist and a hardheaded, adroit, at times cunning politician; a rhetorician, whose elegant phrases had propulsive power, and a no-nonsense administrator—who, above all others, was fated to confront the ambiguities of the Enlightenment program. He had caught a vision, as a precocious leader of the American Revolution, of a comprehensive Enlightenment ideal, a glimpse of what a wholly enlightened world might be, and strove to make it real, discovering as he did so the intractable dilemmas. Repeatedly he saw a pure vision, conceptualized and verbalized it brilliantly, and then struggled to relate it to reality, shifting, twisting, maneuvering backward and forward as he did so.

From the start, and unswervingly, he argued that government must be stripped of its self-justifying power and reduced to an instrument of the people, whose voice could only be that of the majority: "the will of the majority," he said again and again, "ought to be the law." Madison too hoped that the people, not the government as such, would ultimately rule, but he believed that legislative majoritarianism could quickly lead to the destruction of the rights of minorities. For Jefferson the solution was clear: a bill of rights, which he advocated from the moment he first saw the Constitution. "A bill of rights," he wrote, "is what the people are entitled to against every government on earth . . . and what no just government should refuse or rest on inference." But Madison—who in the end would write the national Bill of Rights—pointed out to Jefferson that a limited enumeration of human rights would never prevent anyone from misusing power. Only structural balances within a government, Madison thought, pitting one force against another, could keep the misuse of power in check and so protect minority rights. Ten years later, Jefferson used the same idea in drafting the Kentucky Resolutions, which aimed to protect individual interests by pitting the states against the nation, almost to the point of nullification. But then, shortly thereafter, as president, he overrode the states' rights he had earlier defended, in order to protect the nation, first from subversion, then from the dangers of foreign wars.[13]

Why the inconsistency? There are times, he explained, when the rule of law itself must be suspended:

> A strict observance of the written law is doubtless *one* of the high duties of a good citizen, but it is not *the highest*. The laws of necessity, or self-preservation, of saving our country when in danger, are of higher obligation.[14]

All men, he had written in his most famous pronouncement, are created equal—then why not black slaves? He agonized over the glaring, obvious inconsistency, came back again and again to the bizarre anomaly of slavery in a free state—anomaly in law, in ideology, in simple justice and humanity. His loathing of slavery was sincere, and he predicted that since "God is just [and] . . . his justice cannot sleep forever" it would one day, somehow, disappear from the face of the earth. What, besides his own personal interest, kept him, initially, from developing his early interest in abolition was what seemed to him to be the crippling paradox that freeing the slaves would imperil the survival of the nation's freedom. The blacks, a majority of the population in parts of the South, lacked the qualities, Jefferson believed, that were needed to guarantee the survival of freedom: education, experience in self-government, economic independence. Whether they would ever be able to acquire these requisites of republican citizenship—whether, if their present degraded circumstances were improved and if they were "equally cultivated for a few generations," they would become the equals of any others— was a question that led him into a deeply troubling, unsure racism. What was clear in his mind was that the agrarian South—free of commercial, industrial, and urban corruption—was the bastion of the free republican nation. Black majority rule there would simply overwhelm the freedoms for which he struggled. "Justice is in one scale," he wrote, "and self-preservation in the other."[15]

The problem did not diminish in time; it grew worse. Once, in the hope of at least containing slavery, Jefferson had favored limiting its geographical spread, and in fact he was largely responsible for prohibiting it in the states of the Old Northwest. But later, fearing that the growing congressional power of northern industrial and financial forces would overwhelm the country and destroy the delicate compromises of the Constitution, he changed his mind and supported the expansion of the institution, which he continued to despise and condemn, into Missouri and eventually other states in the South.[16]

Jefferson's fear of northern economic power which propelled this strange reversal flowed from his undiminished commitment to the ideology of the Revolution in its original, pristine form. He had no need to calculate the precise political and social costs and benefits of Hamilton's financial program. He understood the threatening implications immediately; they squared perfectly with his historical memory and his political beliefs and fears. He, like radical theorists in Britain, believed it had all happened before, early in the century, in Walpole's buildup of the power of the British Treasury in collaboration with Britain's new, high-flying, ruthless banking and commercial interests. That alliance, he knew, had allowed Walpole to buy the votes he needed in the House of Commons, overthrow the famed separation of powers of the government, and usher in an age of limitless greed and political squalor.[17]

Jefferson explained this, and its relevance to Hamilton, in his autobiographical miscellany, the *Anas*. In it he recalled his return to the United States in 1789 to become secretary of state, and his shocked discovery of Hamilton's plan for the federal government to assume the debts of the states. There was no mistaking Hamilton's purpose, Jefferson wrote. Hamilton's plan would pump money into the hands of profiteering state creditors in order to pile up "additional recruits" to the "phalanx of the Treasury." And that was not the end of the plans of the "stock-jobbing herd." Though Hamilton and his "votaries" had already become—as Walpole had been—"master of every vote in the legislature . . . the machine was not compleat . . . Some engine of influence more permanent must be contrived," and that engine was the Bank of the United States.

Jefferson feared the bank and fought it from the start. Aside from its probable issuance of a flood of paper money that would lead to wild speculation and to the creation of a "moneyed aristocracy," and aside from its encouraging long-term national indebtedness that would in time burden the living with the extravagance of the dead, he feared the bank's political influence. He knew the historical antecedents. The bank's stockholders, like those of the Bank of England, would forever be able to manufacture a legislative majority to suit them and so corrupt the Constitution and reshape it "on the model of England." He had no choice but to fight this scheme—fight once again precisely the battle that had been fought and lost in England. The parallels were unmistakable. Hamilton, Jefferson concluded, favored monarchy "bottomed on corruption," and he made no bones about it. If you eliminated all the corruption in the British government, Hamilton said in a dinner conversation that Jefferson recalled verbatim, "it would become an *impracticable* government: as it stands at present, with all its supposed defects, it is the most perfect government which ever existed." Hamilton truly believed, Jefferson wrote, "that corruption was essential to the government of a nation," even though the whole history of eighteenth-century Britain, the whole history of Europe, revealed what consequences this kind of corruption could have.[18]

The evils of Hamilton's program and the devastating threat it posed to the nation's freedom were clear to Jefferson from the moment he returned from France. But Hamilton's immediate goal, however erroneously and dangerously pursued, was to stimulate American economic growth, and this was something that Jefferson himself increasingly supported. His republicanism had never been naively "classical" to the exclusion of vigorous economic development or of what has been called possessive individualism, nor did his emphasis on civic virtue preclude the basic value of personal property, its preservation and enhancement. Gradually he came to value—if not the full range of entrepreneurial efforts that Hamilton had earlier promoted, or his methods—policies strangely similar to those of the Federalists. He clung to his major premise, but faced realistically the rapid shifts of the economy, and made a series of adjustments.

Convinced always that "those who labour in the earth are the chosen people of God . . . the most virtuous citizens and possess the most *amor patriae*," and that the survival of freedom depends on them, he began as a radical agrarian, hoping to avoid the corruption of a debased working class and urban slums, and content for the nation to trade staples for the manufactures of others. That led him to a policy of free trade. But then he found that commercial reciprocity was not forthcoming, and so he favored, first, commercial retaliation, then protectionism, and finally the encouragement of domestic manufactures. By 1816 he concurred in a protective tariff, and wrote that "we must now place the manufacturer by the side of the agriculturist." If one did not, the results would be fatal:

> He . . . who is now against domestic manufacture must be for reducing us either to dependence on [the economies of] foreign nation[s] or to be clothed in skins, and to live like wild beasts in dens and caverns. I am not one of these; experience has taught me that manufactures are now as necessary to our independence as to our comfort.[19]

But if that was the case, had not Hamilton's economic policies, which Jefferson had so passionately denounced, been correct from the start? He struggled to square his evolving economic views with the original principles of the Revolution that continued to dominate his thought. So he accepted manufactures; they had become necessary—but let it be *household* manufactures, he said, to keep the units small. An expanded economic role of government? Yes, but let it be chiefly the governments of the states, and the federal government only by constitutional amendment. A national bank? Perhaps: as Madison had seen when he chartered the Second United States Bank, cumulative precedent and popular usage over the years had given the bank a sanction that could not be ignored. But let it issue, not paper currency—which was "only the ghost of money," Jefferson said, "and not money itself" and which would breed speculative crazes and devastating inflation—but bills of credit and Treasury notes that would be quickly redeemed.[20]

A highly pragmatic, tough-minded, and successful politician, Jefferson never abandoned the ideals he had so brilliantly expressed in the years before independence, and he struggled endlessly with the ambiguities they posed. Testing, probing constantly, he sought in every way he could to contain the real world in the embrace of his utopian ideals.

The press, he eloquently insisted, must always be free. On this he could not have been more flatly assertive, more unambiguously clear. "Our liberty depends on the freedom of the press," he wrote, "and that cannot be limited without being lost." Again: "Where the press is free, and every man able to read, all is safe." And again, most famously: "Were it left to me to decide whether we should have a government without newspapers or newspapers without a government, I should not hesitate a moment to prefer the latter." But were there *no* limits to the freedom of the press? Yes, in fact, there were. Drawing unquestioningly on the received, libertarian tradition of the early eighteenth century, which was bound into the ideology of the Revolution, he assumed that while one could print anything one wanted to print, one was liable to legal prosecution "for false facts printed and published." But the question, he discovered in his years in power, was what, in matters of political opinion, is true and what is false. Who is to judge, and by what criteria? Why did not the "overt acts" doctrine of his Act for Establishing Religious Freedom apply in secular matters? Why would not his enemies' political falsehoods be as certainly defeated by truth as he had said false religious beliefs would be? Jefferson, reacting furiously to political attacks, adhered to his original view, which criminalized false statements, only to find himself forced to question his own basic premises. In the heat of party struggles he could only doubt, despondently, that truth could ever emerge from the contest between what he took to be an utterly ruthless, lying, scurrilous opposition press and his own right-minded publicists. At the end of his presidency he wrote that outright suppression of the press would be no more injurious to the public good than the newspapers' "abandoned prostitution to falsehood."[21]

This was not, of course, his normal stance. He truly wished for free speech and a free press; but the complexity of these liberal goals, their inner ambiguities in application, came to him only gradually.

In the mid 1780s, recognizing the weakness and inefficiency of the federal government, he shared the view that the Articles of Confederation would have to be strengthened, but only in a few specified ways. His immediate reaction to the new Constitution when it reached him in Paris was strongly negative: its far-reaching provisions "stagger all my dispositions to subscribe" to it. "All the good of this new constitution," he wrote, "might have been couched in three or four new articles to be added to the good, old, and venerable fabrick, which should have been preserved even as a religious relique." Fearing, ever, the possible re-creation of monarchy in a new guise, he was certain that a president who *could* be re-elected repeatedly, *would* be, and the result would be "a bad edition of a Polish king." Madison, who had worried through every clause and phrase of the Constitution in the most critical way possible, wrote Jefferson, on October 24, 1787, a long, searching analysis of the drafting and character of the Constitution. In it Madison argued that an increase in the size of a republic, far from endangering freedom by requiring an excess of power to keep order and to enforce the laws, would in fact protect freedom by dissipating animosities and multiplying factions to the point that no one interest could control the government. But Jefferson, in his reply, did not comment on, if he grasped, this counterintuitive idea; he reverted to the traditional fear of monarchy, elective or hereditary. Think of the Roman emperors, he wrote Madison in commenting on presidential power, think of the popes, the German emperors, the deys of the Ottoman dependencies, the Polish kings—all of them elective in some sense. "An incapacity to be elected [president] a second time would have been the only effective preventative," he said. "The king of Poland is removable every day by the Diet, yet he is never removed."[22]

Such was Jefferson's immediate reaction to the Constitution. But soon, characteristically, as he studied the ways the Constitution would actually work, he transcended this initial response and began to recognize the document's virtues. Within a few weeks he saw enough good in the Constitution to declare himself "nearly a neutral" on ratification. Soon thereafter he said he hoped that the requisite nine states would ratify, thus putting the Constitution into effect, but that the other four should hold out until amendments were made. Finally, after conferring with Lafayette and Paine, and convinced that the states' *recommended* amendments would quickly be enacted, he declared that outright ratification was "absolutely necessary" and that the American Constitution was "unquestionably the wisest ever yet presented to men." "We can surely boast," he concluded, "of having set the world a beautiful example of a government reformed by reason alone, without bloodshed."[23]

So, gradually Jefferson came to accept the Constitution's basic propositions: that power could be created and constrained at the same time; that internal balances between essential rights and necessary powers could be so constructed as to be self-sustaining; that the power of a centralized, national, self-financing state could be compatible with the safety and freedom of ordinary people. The mechanics of this plan had not been the product of a grand theory.

No one had designed the Constitution. It had been arrived at by a complex process of adjustments, balances, compromises, and modifications. And therefore it is perhaps more surprising that Jefferson came so fully to accept the Constitution, and later himself to use so skillfully the executive powers that it created, than that he opposed it when it first appeared.

For the fear of power—the very heart of the original Revolutionary ideology—was an animating spirit behind all of his thinking, and ultimately the source of the deepest ambiguities. Though as president he never hesitated to use the full authority of his office, at times to use powers his opponents claimed he had no constitutional right to use, he never ceased believing that the only truly free governments were small ward-level units in which power scarcely existed and in which ordinary citizens could easily participate in government.[24]

He struggled to eliminate aristocracies of birth and inherited wealth because, he believed, they inevitably created arbitrary power—irrational and unjustifiable power that, as he saw so vividly in Europe, could crush every impulse of ordinary people's desire for self-fulfillment. The evils of hereditary power profoundly moved him, and propelled his eloquence to extraordinary heights. In America, he wrote from France, there had never been legal distinctions among freemen "by birth or badge." Of such distinctions, "they had no more idea than they had of the mode of existence in the moon or planets." But in Europe the full horror of aristocracies of birth could be seen on every side. It was a world, Jefferson wrote,

> where the dignity of man is lost in arbitrary distinctions, where the human species is classed into several stages of degradation, where the many are crouched under the weight of the few, and where the order established can present to the contemplation of a thinking being no other picture than that of God almighty and his angels trampling under foot the hosts of the damned.[25]

But Jefferson was an aristocrat himself. He enjoyed an inheritance of lands and slaves, and he shared the planter class's fear of mobs and of the rule of mass democracy. Salvation, for him, lay in the rule of *natural* aristocracies, elites of talent and wisdom, devoted to the public good. But he recognized that in America as in Europe the leisure and education that nurtured talent were traditionally products of inherited wealth. It followed therefore, by a logic he found compelling all his life, that a massive, systematic structure of public education that would identify and nourish native talent would be necessary if America were to retain its freedom.

His Bill for the More General Diffusion of Knowledge (1779) he always considered one of his most important contributions to the comprehensive revision of Virginia's laws, and he never ceased hoping that its provisions would be enacted and reproduced on a national scale. But they were not. Even in Virginia he was defeated— by parsimonious legislators; by the parochial interests of religious denominations; and by the popularity of what he called "petty *academies*" that seemed to be springing up on all sides and that inculcated in students, he said, "just taste enough of learning to be alienated from industrious pursuits, and not enough to do service in the ranks of science." Public education, "to bring into action that mass of talents which lie buried in poverty in every country, for want of the means of development," was an essential means of eliminating arbitrary power. The provision in Spain's short-lived, liberal constitution of 1812 that literacy would be a prerequisite for citizenship excited his greatest admiration. "Enlighten the people generally," he said, "and tyranny and oppressions of body and mind will vanish like evil spirits at the dawn of day." But he did not live to see that dawn, nor could he conceive that a strange, unsystematic melange of schools— public and private, parochial and secular—would one day create the universal education he so passionately desired.[26]

Similarly, he opposed political parties, on principle, because he believed that organized political machines generated arbitrary power, power for partisan groups—selfish, power-hungry cliques, which inevitably violated the public interest. It was therefore logical for him to declare, after the bitter presidential election of 1800, that "we are all republicans; we are all federalists," since he could only think of the Federalist Party not as a legitimate ruling body that differed from the Republicans on matters of policy, but as a malevolent junta (a "herd of traitors," he called them) who dreamed of "a single and splendid government of an aristocracy, founded on banking institutions and moneyed incorporations . . . riding and ruling over the plundered ploughman and beggared yeomanry." Once the Federalist leaders were driven from office, their followers would naturally, Jefferson believed, join the national—that is, Republican—majority. But parties survived, and for that Jefferson himself was largely responsible. To destroy the Federalist Party he had had no choice but to create his own, more effective party, with devoted cadres, good organization, and an articulated program. In the process he did much, modern historians agree, "to engrain into American political life the party system, to make party government acceptable, to make party machinery a normal part of political activity, [and] to make party and patronage inseparable."[27]

His hatred of poverty, too, was rooted in his elemental fear of arbitrary power. If he had not known from history that ignorant, idle, impoverished people were always the helpless tools of demagogues, he would have discovered it in his years in Europe. In general, his experiences there confirmed his ideological commitments, and none more than his belief that economic debasement and political tyranny go hand in hand.

He was horrified by the poverty he saw in France. A casual encounter with a beggar woman outside Fontainebleau, her tears of gratitude for the few coins he gave her, touched off "a train of reflections on [the] unequal division of property." The wealth of France, he wrote Madison, "is absolutely concentrated in a very few hands." The grandees employ "the flower of the country as servants," leaving the masses unemployed—begging and desperate—while vast lands are set aside as game preserves. He was well aware, he wrote, "that an equal division of property is impracticable," but the staggering inequality he was witnessing created such misery that, for the preservation of freedom if not for simple justice, every effort must be made legally to subdivide inherited property and to distribute it equally among descendants.[28]

It had been for that reason in 1776 that he had written the law abolishing primogeniture and entail in Virginia, and in his draft constitution for the state he had stipulated that "every person of full age" who did not own fifty acres of land would be entitled to that amount from the public domain.[29] The earth, he said again and again, by natural right belongs to the living and not to the dead or to their privileged descendants. Where, as in France, huge territories owned by the few are left wild while masses starve, natural right is violated, and in time those deprived of that right may well lay claim to it in ways no responsible person would favor. Poverty, Jefferson believed, was thus a political as well as a social curse; it was the foundation of an unjust concentration of political power, and led inevitably to the destruction of freedom. But he had no program for preventing the growth of poverty or for abolishing it where it existed. And he was repeatedly attacked for promoting policies that depressed the economic well-being of whole regions, chief among them his embargo of 1807–8.

That policy was devised and sustained by his idealistic passion for rational solutions to international conflicts, but it proved to profit the rich and the unscrupulous while sacrificing the welfare of the poor. His critics were relentless. New England and the middle states, they charged, deprived of commerce and overseas markets, were devastated, but at least they could find partial relief in manufactures for a protected home market. The South, however, and Jefferson's own state in particular, had no such means of relief. "Tobacco was worthless," Henry Adams would write, relishing the irony of Jefferson's presidency in a brilliant passage of his *History*,

> but four hundred thousand negro slaves must be clothed and fed, great establishments must be kept up, [and] the social scale of living could not be reduced . . . With astonishing rapidity Virginia succumbed to ruin, while continuing to support the system that was draining her strength. No episode in American history was more touching than the generous devotion with which Virginia clung to the embargo, and drained the poison which her own President held obstinately to her lips . . . The old society of Virginia could never be restored. Amid the harsh warnings of John Randolph it saw its agonies approach; and its last representative, heir

to all its honors and dignities, President Jefferson himself woke from his long dream of power only to find his own fortunes buried in the ruin he had made.[30]

Fearing concentrations of power, and arbitrary power of any kind, convinced that America's experimental achievements in freedom were beset by forces that would destroy them—but endowed, himself, with an instinct for power and with exceptional political and administrative skills, and blessed with many years of active life in politics—Jefferson, more than any other of the Revolution's original leaders, explored the ambiguities of freedom. If the principles that had emerged in the great struggle with Britain before 1776 had not been so clear, so luminous and compelling, in his mind; or if he had remained on the sidelines, commenting like a Greek chorus on the great events of the day, the world would have been simpler for him, the ambiguities less painful, and his reputation less complicated. As it was, he remained throughout his long career the clear voice of America's Revolutionary ideology, its purest conscience, its most brilliant expositor, while struggling to deal with the intractable mass of the developing nation's everyday problems. In this double role— ideologist and practical politician, theorist and pragmatist—he sought to realize the Revolution's glittering promise, and as he did so he discovered the inner complexities and ambiguities of these ideals as well as their strengths, and left a legacy of compromise and incompleteness which his critics would forever assail.

It was an endless struggle. He never ceased to fear that the great experiment might fail, that the United States might be torn apart by its internal divisions or overwhelmed by the pressures of the outside world and, like so many other nations, in the end forfeit its freedom for a specious security. But he did not despair. He hoped, with increasing confidence, that the common sense of the people and their innate idealism would overcome the obstacles and somehow resolve the ambiguities, and that America would fulfill its destiny— which was, he believed, to preserve, and to extend to other regions of the earth, "the sacred fire of freedom and self-government," and to liberate the human mind from every form of tyranny.[31]

# III

# Realism and Idealism in
# American Diplomacy:
# Franklin in Paris, *Couronné par la Liberté*

That Felix Gilbert, a German-born and German-educated historian of Renaissance Italy and Prussian politics should have published *To the Farewell Address: Ideas of Early American Foreign Policy* (1961) is one of the least likely events in American historiography. That slim volume set the terms for an extended debate not only on the original character of American diplomacy but on the general nature of America's role in world affairs. Yet, unlikely as it may seem, Gilbert's background prepared him uniquely for this influential foray into American history and for the challenging view it contained.

Scion of a German family prominent in cultural and financial life, Gilbert (1905–1991) had been named after his great-grandfather, the composer Felix Mendelssohn, and was closely related to the cultivated bankers, industrialists, and officials in the Mendelssohn-Bartholdy-Oppenheim clan.[1] He had been educated at Heidelberg and had served a rigorous scholar's apprenticeship, first in Berlin under Friedrich Meinecke, who directed his doctoral dissertation on the nineteenth-century historian Johann Gustav Droysen, then, under the supervision of his uncle Albrecht Mendelssohn Bartholdy, as assistant in the great documentary project in German foreign policy, *Die Grosse Politik der Europäischen Kabinette*. He had turned thereafter to Renaissance studies, devoting himself to the balance of power in fifteenth- and sixteenth-century Italy and to the historiography of Machiavelli and Guicciardini. Had the upheaval of Nazism and World War II not interrupted his promising academic career, he would have remained in Germany and Italy, refining and developing his studies of the Renaissance and nineteenth-century German politics. In later years he would resume those studies, but only after a significant detour.

With fascist pressure bearing down on him, Gilbert migrated, first to England and then to America, where in 1939 his talents were recognized by an appointment as a member of the Institute for Advanced Study in Princeton. There he joined a special seminar on American foreign policy that had been convened within a month of the outbreak of World War II to analyze the history of isolationism in American life and the nation's traditional fear of "entangling alliances." Some of the finest minds in American historical, political, and cultural scholarship came together in that group to probe this bitterly divisive topic, which was convulsing American politics as war swept over Europe. Everyone knew that America's stance toward the world conflict would shape the fate of Western civilization, but in 1939–40 isolationism remained dominant. Why? What was the source and character of this desire to withdraw from transatlantic affairs? How deep did it run in American life? What status did it, or should it, have in contemporary American life?

In the research and papers Gilbert presented to the seminar he sought to trace America's isolationism back to its historical roots and thus to grasp its essence. Anticipations could be found, he wrote, in Thomas Paine's pamphlet *Common Sense*, which so greatly stimulated the movement for American independence, and in commonplace discussions in American coffeehouses and political meetings. But mainly, Gilbert concluded in his work for the seminar, the idea originated in the British mindset, the British stance toward Europe, which Paine and others brought with them to America. By July 1940 the seminar's leader could report that Gilbert, "in several careful studies" which constituted "an original and unique contribution to

American history," had shown the importance of Britain's fear of continental entanglements in the eighteenth century and the peculiar and profound way that fear shaped American thinking. It formed the background to Washington's Farewell Address and fed American suspicions of the process of diplomacy itself. In October 1940 Gilbert's book on the subject was said to be ready for publication by Christmas.[2]

In fact the book appeared only after Gilbert had had twenty more years of experience in the United States and after World War II had been fought and concluded and one could take a longer view of the course of American foreign policy in the light of the Cold War.[3] By 1961 the initial concerns of 1939–40 still lay at the heart of Gilbert's thinking, but the emphasis had shifted and broadened. At the core of the book now lay the complex proposition that American culture had had from the start "a strong feeling of material realism and a pervasive air of utopian idealism and, consequently, two different attitudes regarding the Old World: attraction and rejection." What struck Gilbert most forcefully as he examined the founding of the American nation in the context of his studies of nineteenth-century Prussian politics, Machiavelli, the balance of power in and among the Renaissance states, and the failure of the Revolution of 1848 was the persistent strain of idealism in American public life— indeed, its utopian idealism, latent or manifest. The European roots of American isolationism could easily be demonstrated, but isolationism in America could also and perhaps more significantly be seen as a defensive policy to protect utopian hopes that a better world, freer, less subject to the misuse of power than heretofore, could be built on this continent if the new nation kept itself free of the devastation of Europe's power struggles. America's basic attitude to foreign policy, Gilbert wrote in the conclusion of the book, was shaped by

the tension between Idealism and Realism. Settled by men who looked for gain and by men who sought freedom, born into independence in a century of enlightened thinking and of power politics, America has wavered in her foreign policy between Idealism and Realism, and her great historical moments have occurred when both were combined.[4]

This was the essence of Gilbert's view, the fruit of his research for the Institute's remarkable seminar and of twenty-five years of involvement in American life. But the book is not simply an essay in abstractions. It focuses on the importance of a single document, the Continental Congress's draft treaty of 1776, which John Adams took with him to Europe as a formula for the diplomatic alliances he was instructed to make for the embattled new nation. Gilbert viewed that document as an effort to establish American foreign relations on the basis of a new idealism in the relations among states, on sheer rationality, not on power politics. Behind it lay the enlightened conviction that the free flow of commerce between nations would be advantageous to all, that neutral carriers should have freedom of the seas in times of war, that the definition of contraband should be severely limited, and that there should be complete reciprocity in commercial rights and privileges between the inhabitants of the contracting powers. Adams, Gilbert explains, attempted to conclude treaties in the spirit of this draft, which would have established a degree of freedom and equality among nations "which would eliminate all cause for tension and political conflicts," but in this he largely failed. Adams came to realize that the passion for power, for domination over others, would always prevail over ideals, and that, as a consequence, hardheaded realism alone could guarantee America's survival. But despite Adams's disillusion, Gilbert concluded, the strain of idealism embedded in the draft treaty survived, and found one of its most resounding expressions in Washington's Farewell Address.[5]

The debate Gilbert's book touched off has not yet subsided. An entire volume has been devoted to challenging his interpretation of the draft treaty, and several articles extend the criticism.[6] But however one interprets the details of the draft treaty, and however tough-minded and pragmatic Adams and his colleagues can be shown in fact to have become, in a larger and deeper sense Gilbert was right.

He had a powerful point of comparison, which American historians lacked. He knew what the politics of Europe had been; he knew what Machiavellianism could lead to; and he, like every one of the Hitler refugees, knew only too well what unconstrained power could mean in its most brutal forms. Yes, American politicians were, or became, realists, but for him what stood out in America's Revolutionary history was not the opportunism and self-interest of the nation's new leaders, but their idealism, their determination to restrain the misuse of power and to protect the individual from an overmighty state.

Gilbert's sources were limited. His focus was concentrated on diplomacy. But he could have found a hundred expressions of his theme in the broader history of the Revolution. He centered his discussion on Adams because Adams played a vital role in writing the draft treaty, which he felt expressed America's original aims in diplomacy, and was entrusted with the task of concluding treaties in Europe. But Adams was only one of a team of diplomats the United States sent to Europe in the 1770s, and the key figure, flamboyantly successful, was Benjamin Franklin, commissioner, then minister plenipotentiary, in France throughout most of the decade after 1776.

The two men, Adams and Franklin, were forced by fate and the Continental Congress to collaborate in negotiations abroad, and an odder couple never existed. Adams was an introspective, self-conscious, awkward, driven, fiercely dutiful, upright neo-Puritan— lacking, his old friend Mercy Otis Warren wrote in her history of the American Revolution, in the "*je ne scai quoi*" necessary to succeed in European society. He was never a politician—never, as he confessed, practiced "in intrigues for power." Sensitive to insults, imaginary and real, he felt the world was generally hostile, to himself and to the American cause, which was the great passion of his life. There were enemies on all sides. Even the French, supposedly America's allies, he believed, were determined "to prevent the growth of our people . . . Gratitude to France is the greatest of follies," and, Franklin reported of Adams's views, "to be influenced by it, would ruin us." Which led Franklin, who correctly gauged the workings of French diplomacy, to say of Adams that "he means well for his country, is always an honest man, often a wise one, but sometimes and in some things absolutely out of his senses."[7]

Franklin's despair of his colleague's judgment and behavior was warmly reciprocated. The two men had met before they joined forces in Paris, most intimately in 1776, as representatives to the so-called Staten Island Peace Conference. At that makeshift, futile meeting, accommodations had been such that they had had to share a bed, an event Adams recorded with good humor—how he had failed to get that "old conjuror," that "Egyptian mummy," to shut the window, and how he had fallen asleep when Franklin began lecturing him "upon air and cold and respiration and perspiration." But now, in Paris, the issues were deadly serious. What was Adams to make of Franklin's behavior? The world famous scientist and writer was seventy in 1777 when he settled into Paris, where, on two previous visits, he had already been celebrated as a *philosophe,* savant, and legislator—and "as a kind of living document from America." Now, a member of the French Royal Academy and the embodiment of America's enlightened Revolution, he quickly became the rage of Parisian high society and the toast of the cognoscenti all over Europe. The Paris salons were entranced by him. The most sophisticated women literally hung on his neck, wrote poems to him, sent him, and received back from him, bantering love letters. His writings were published and republished. His portrait was painted and reproduced in prints endlessly; his face appeared everywhere—on medallions, vases, rings, dishware, snuffboxes. So familiar was his name, Adams recalled, that "there was scarcely a peasant or a citizen, a *valet de chambre,* coachman or footman, a lady's chambermaid or a scullion in a kitchen, who was not familiar with it, and who did not consider him as a friend to human kind. When they spoke of him, they seemed to think he was to restore the golden age."[8]

Franklin's fame, his untroubled high spirits, his gaiety and wit, his social success, and above all his casual insouciance and apparent indolence drove Adams into fits of frustration. Franklin, he came to believe, was corrupt, both morally and politically. The great man, Adams recalled in his autobiography, slept late, and when he managed to finish breakfast he was surrounded by all sorts of odd types, "phylosophers, accademicians and economists . . . atheists, deists, and libertines," and by crowds of women and children who flocked around just to look at him, "and to have the pleasure of telling stories about his simplicity, his bald head, and scattering gray hair." Eventually, Adams reported, they would all amble off to dinner and the theatre and an evening of chatter in the salons.[9]

As far as Adams could see, Franklin did very little work, and what he did was done with an appalling lack of secrecy. Versailles was a snake pit of intrigue, and Franklin's desk, Adams said, was a regular sieve. In fact, it was worse than he knew. We know—he did not—that the secretary of the American delegation, Edward Bancroft, in addition to being a crooked speculator in arms shipments and stock markets, was a British spy. Undetected, leaving documents for the British ambassador in the hole of a tree on the south side of the Tuileries, he sent so much secret information over to London that it became an embarrassment to British intelligence. One highly confidential memorial from the American commissioners to the French foreign secretary, Vergennes, was protested by the British ambassador before Vergennes had heard of it. But Franklin seemed not to care. His rule, he wrote one of the people who warned him that he was "surrounded *with spies,* who watch your every movement," was to do nothing shameful, "nothing but what spies may see and welcome." The more one's honorable actions were known, he wrote, the better for all. "If I was sure therefore that my valet de place was a spy, as probably he is, I think I should not discharge him for that, if in other respects I lik'd him."[10]

Adams was shocked by such bland and righteous innocence. He could not believe it was sincere, hence it was highly suspicious—and then, to compound the mystery of Franklin's behavior, it all seemed to work to America's advantage. The loose flow of information from Franklin to Britain's secret service suggested to the French, who could not believe Franklin was not deliberately leaking such confidential documents, that he was conniving with the British and might soon come to terms with them. The French, who were determined not to let this happen, were therefore encouraged to support America's war for independence or lose the great opportunity to take revenge on Britain for the defeats of the Seven Years' War. At the same time the British actually read the dispatches, and realized how close the coordination of French and American policy was, and so they got the impression, heightened by France's public celebration of Franklin, that America and France were on the verge of an alliance, and that therefore England should not commit itself totally to the American conflict with a major war with France lurking over the horizon.[11]

So Franklin's slack behavior became an adroit maneuver—half contrived, half the lucky product of his casual ways—which strengthened France's support of America while it inhibited Britain's war effort.

Franklin could not have been more Machiavellian, shrewder in playing both ends off against the middle, or more skillful in exploiting the balance of power. But America's great historical moments—and the establishment of the nation's independence was the greatest of all—have occurred when realism and idealism have been combined, and no one knew this better than Franklin. He knew that America had a unique and powerful meaning for the enlightened reformers of France, and that he himself, his very existence, was the embodiment, the palpable expression, of that meaning.

British North America had long been the subject of intense scrutiny by European thinkers—partly out of interest in the effect of environment on human development, but mainly out of the need for proof of what a society of Europeans would be like if the burdens of European establishments were radically reformed or eliminated: if powerful established churches, with their priesthoods and wealth and inquisitions, were eliminated; if feudal landowning, which gave great wealth, leisure, and power to a few and guaranteed poverty for the masses, were abolished; and if oppressive economies, bound down by medieval restrictions and encumbrances, were rationalized and modernized. In America the enlightened reformers believed they had found the answers, and answers that gave the lie to conservatives who argued that the powerful institutions of the ancien régime alone protected Europe from barbarism, that if the structure of civilization as it was known were eliminated the result would not be Elysium but savagery. America, the *philosophes,* and especially Voltaire, said, was there to prove the opposite. And the very embodiment of America, hence of the idealistic hopes of the Enlightenment, was Franklin—a backwoods autodidact, nature's philosopher, who had become one of the world's great scientists, belletrists, and diplomats.[12] Everything about him was important, and especially his manner and physical appearance, which in themselves, as Franklin knew very well, became a vital part of the Enlightenment's reform ideology. Gradually over the years—by a remarkable process of symbolic accommodation—his physical image, represented in many forms, shifted to express these aspirations, his own as well as those of Europe's *philosophes.*

He had always been conscious of his image and its meaning, and had knowingly shaped it—not cynically, not to deceive, but spontaneously, to express his own view of himself as his roles developed and his activities expanded. Like most self-made men, he was aware of himself and knew the effect he was having—and never more so than when he moved, with increasing confidence, into the Parisian core of the enlightened world.

He had not always had such access, and he responded with the heightened zest of the once-deprived. In the sixteen years he had spent in England as agent for various American constituencies he had circulated among the intelligentsia and the middle-class literati—printers, newspaper writers, clerics, merchants, scientists, and free thinkers: he was at home in the Club of Honest Whigs and the Royal Society. But the ruling aristocracy, the power brokers, and the leaders of high fashion had been beyond his reach. One of the most famous men of his day, accomplished in science, letters, and politics, and quietly dignified, but without wealth, or rank, or power, he had been obliged to hang about the antechambers of the great, soliciting audiences. Twice he had been cruelly humiliated—by the secretary of state for the colonies, who rejected his credentials and went out of his way to insult him, and, notoriously, by the solicitor general in a public denunciation in the Privy Council, during which Franklin stood mute and which he left burning with anger and frustration.[13] But now, in Paris, the world had changed. It was he who was solicited, not only by the publicists and literati but also by the rich, the noble, the leaders of fashion, at times by men of power. He responded happily, joyously, spontaneously—reaching, as he did, a new level of self-realization, which he expressed not only verbally but visually.[14]

Visual portrayals of his self-awareness were nothing new. Thirty years earlier he had first presented himself visually, in a portrait that expresses accurately his sense of his earliest achievements [fig. 41]. Painted by the self-taught mariner-artist Robert Feke around 1746, when Franklin had just retired from business to devote himself to science and public affairs, it conveys perfectly the calm, self-confident, unostentatious persona of the successful small businessman. The coat and waistcoat are dark and inconspicuous, the hat is stiffly held in the crook of the elbow, the linen, prominently displayed, is only modestly stylish, and the wig, though clearly a sign of respectability, is a rather old-fashioned cap of brown curls each of which is highlighted to give a burnished, somewhat glowing appearance. There is no adornment; the pursed lips are expressionless; no message is conveyed except that the sitter has arrived. Even the background is silent: featureless gray clouds and empty hills vaguely fill out the picture. The one mildly dramatic feature—the rather elegant, delicately pointing fingers of the right hand, curiously reminiscent of statues of the winged Mercury—seems out of place, incongruous in this calm, erect figure of bourgeois stolidity.

Sixteen years later—long a resident of London, famed for his achievements in science, his literary skills, and his political prominence—Franklin recast his image. The successful tradesman is left behind, and in two major portraits he emerges as the consummate man of science, the experimenter, the thinker, the ultimate *philosophe*.

The Mason Chamberlin portrait (1762), whose details are here

Fig. 41

highlighted in the mid-nineteenth-century copy by Leslie [fig. 42], shows the abstracted, devoted student of science, the experimental observer, gazing intently not at the powerful, destructive storm, visible through the window on Franklin's left, but at the lightning's activation of the electrical apparatus on his right—wires and bells— whose motions Franklin, pen in hand, is about to record. The face is calm, the lips characteristically pursed, and the clothes still dark and plain, though the wig is now that of a man of substance, a professional of some distinction and status. Franklin liked this picture of

Fig. 42

himself as a man of science; it was promptly engraved and the prints were widely distributed. It was re-engraved a decade later, for a frontispiece to a French translation of Franklin's writings, and so it was in this form that Franklin's image first appeared in French prints.

But a second portrait of the London years appealed to Franklin even more. In the portrait by David Martin of 1766 [fig. 43], Franklin is no longer the technical experimenter probing the laws of nature.

Fig. 43

He is now more mature; he wears spectacles low on his nose; he is lost in thought; and he has attained an altogether new level of affluence. Seated in an upholstered chair whose back is decorated with gilded carvings, wearing an elegant powdered wig and a velvet suit with ornamental buttons and gold-braided buttonholes, surrounded by handsome leather-bound volumes, and facing—almost nose-to-nose—a bust of Newton, Franklin, thumb on chin, is the thinker, the calm contemplator of human fate. And yet, at the edges of his mouth there is a smile lurking, suggesting an Erasmian recognition of mankind's folly.

Franklin particularly liked this portrait, its "thoughtfulness, calmness, and reserve." It was, as the painter Allan Ramsay said, a picture of "the *philosopher . . . it seemed to think*," and it was a testimonial to Franklin's achievements of the London years.[15] He had a copy made (with the chair's gilded carvings carefully removed) which he sent home to his wife and left in his will to the Supreme Executive Council of Pennsylvania.

A decade later, on the cusp of his great adventure in Paris, Franklin's persona was once again, and now sensationally, transformed. His actual appearance, as he stepped onto the shore of Brittany early in December 1776 accompanied by his two young grandsons, violated every norm of diplomatic behavior. The wig was gone and in its place was a rather ragged cap of marten fur, whose warmth he had discovered on his trip to Canada some months before; completely covering his head, it fell, in front, down over his brow but left visible, in back, his thin, shoulder-length gray hair. He still wore the silver-rimmed spectacles of the Martin portrait, but his clothes were dark and plain, free of all the earlier ornamentation. Short and stout, he carried only a white walking stick, an almost ironic deviation from the customary sword.[16]

The plain clothes, the fur hat, the spectacles, the stick, the youthful entourage were an unheard-of violation of normal ambassadorial behavior, and they struck the leaders and publicists of a sophisticated nation, whose royal court was almost paralyzed by ritual and protocol, as the unmistakable signs of a dramatic new force in public affairs. Lacking all of the usual symbols of eminence and power, Franklin's appearance, in its very contrariness, became a power in itself. Eminently newsworthy, it entered quickly into mass communication.

Within a few weeks of his arrival in Paris, Franklin's portrait was sketched twice, once by the elderly, accomplished artist Charles Nicolas Cochin, and again by a perceptive amateur, the twenty-two-year-old Thomas Walpole, the son of the English banker who had

BENJAMIN FRANKLIN.

Né à Boston, dans la nouvelle Angleterre le 17 Janvier 1706.

Fig. 44

once worked with Franklin in western land speculation and who now lived in Paris. These hasty, original drawings have not survived, but both became the basis for memorable images that circulated widely within France and then, in innumerable copies and mutations, throughout Europe. Both appealed to the hopes and aspirations of enlightened reformers everywhere; both reflected Franklin's sense of his and his nation's ideal role in world history.

Cochin sent his preliminary drawing to his regular collaborator, Augustin de Saint-Aubin, a distinguished engraver, who produced a print from the quick sketch that proved to be one of the most widely distributed news pictures of the eighteenth century and the most enduring depiction of Franklin as ideologue [fig. 44]. There is no way of tracing the number of copies of the print Cochin and Saint-Aubin sold or distributed, no way of cataloguing the many variations of the print that were made by others, no way even of identifying all the media, the art and craft forms, in which this image appeared. But none of the surviving variations recaptures the force of the original: the strange sidelong glance; the awkward but somehow comfortable fit of the hat and the spectacles; the self-confident, slightly disdainful tight-lipped expression that suggested deep reserves of experience, purpose, and guile. It is an eloquent print which not only bore a message from the New World to the Old that alarmed the state censors, but also tickled the fancy of high society: fashionable women soon began dressing their hair with fur "*à la Franklin*."

The sensational Cochin print was published in early June 1777, six months after Franklin's arrival. Simultaneously, the young Walpole's sketch appeared, in an unexpected form, made possible by Franklin's generous philo-American landlord in Passy, the businessman Donatien Le Ray de Chaumont. Devoted to liberal causes, an early supplier of materiel to the American army, and a great admirer of Franklin, Chaumont sent Walpole's sketch to the artist-manager of his pottery factory, Jean Baptiste Nini, with orders to use it as the basis of a terra-cotta medallion to honor the distinguished American. Nini grappled with the problems presented by Walpole's sketch and produced a series of trials of the bas-relief profile. The fur hat as

Fig. 45

Fig. 46

Fig. 47

Fig. 48

sketched by Walpole or as described to Nini must have defeated him, since he simply copied Rousseau's fur hat as shown in Ramsay's famous portrait of Rousseau and its popular mezzotint reproduction [fig. 45], thereby heightening the ideological effect of the Franklin medallion by creating a visual association between the two men instantly recognizable by the cognoscenti. The spectacles gave him trouble too. In one trial he bent the left bar down sufficiently to reveal the eye [fig. 46]; in the end he gave that up entirely.

Nini's final terra-cotta medallion, with Rousseau's hat and a rather bland, plump Franklin without glasses, bearing under the cut of the shoulder a shield decorated with lightning and thunderbolts [fig. 47], was an enormous success, far greater than Chaumont could have hoped for. It was a sensation when it appeared for sale at a fashionable porcelain exhibit at Versailles, and it appealed to Franklin personally, not only because he liked this comfortable, homey picture of himself but also because he recognized its power in popularizing the American cause. He happily distributed copies to friends in Europe and to family members at home, commenting that with this popular medallion, together with the Cochin print and the variations derived from them, his face had become as well known as that of the moon.

He could not have known how true this was. In the two years that followed, and especially after the American victory at Saratoga in

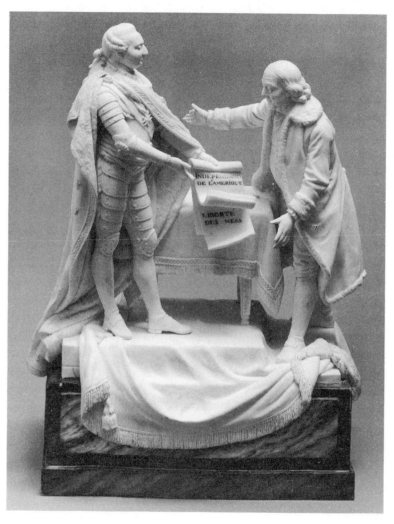

Fig. 49

October 1777 and the Franco-American alliance of February 1778, a veritable avalanche of likenesses appeared, in every conceivable form. From the Sèvres porcelain factory came not only a series of derivative medallions and busts but also china cups with Franklin's portrait painted on the sides, together with saucers decorated with

Fig. 50

symbols of the Franco-American alliance [fig. 48]. From a factory
in Lorraine came a statuette group showing Louis XVI, in armor,
offering Franklin two scrolls, one inscribed "Indépendance de
L'Amerique," the other "Liberté des mers" [fig. 49]. From elsewhere
in France came a glass-cased wooden model of Franklin the scientist
happily at work; the small, beaming doll-like figure, complete with
natural hair and a removable hat, is seated at a table containing an
electrical machine with moving parts [fig. 50]. Later, from Germany,
came a painted wax high relief showing a rather distracted Franklin

Fig. 51

with protruding eyes clutching a large volume to his ornamented robe [fig. 51]. And there would be an enormously popular statuette of Franklin in full figure, sagging rather strangely at the knees, originally produced in terra-cotta, then reproduced in various metals, in marble, in plaster, and in china, "and in every size from miniature to life" [fig. 52].[17]

By then two great sculptors had produced remarkable busts. Jean-Jacques Caffiéri, eager for commissions from the new nation, worked quickly, and completed his bust soon after Franklin's arrival [fig. 53]. Franklin, sitting for the sculptor, had insisted on exactitude, and those who knew him at the time, and Franklin himself, believed it to be the most accurate reproduction of his features ever made. But though there is no deliberate effort at idealization or dramatization, the effect is quietly heroic. It is the realistic, unpretending face of a person of extraordinary solidity of character, inner strength, reserve, and poise. Jean-Antoine Houdon's bust [fig. 54], completed a year after

Fig. 52

Fig. 53

Fig. 54

Caffiéri's and based on casual observation, not direct measurement, is more of a comment, a statement, than Caffiéri's, and more of an effort at popularization. The face is in motion—alert and involved. In Caffiéri's the eyes are caught in an abstracted gaze, in Houdon's the pupils are fixed on a specific object somewhere to the side. In Caffiéri's the mouth is firm, unexpressive, unsmiling; in Houdon's it is partly open as if speaking, and vaguely smiling. In Caffiéri's the hair falls straight; in Houdon's it is drawn, somewhat romantically, back behind the ears. Both are masterly representations, but Caffiéri's is that of dignity abstracted and contained; Houdon's, a fleshier face, is that of a personality engaged. Casts and other reproductions of both were immediately and repeatedly made, but the casts that Franklin bought for his own distribution were those of Caffiéri.

Thus Franklin, seen first as the successful bourgeois, then as the man of science, the intellectual, had become—to Adams's immense chagrin—the embodiment of American idealism and of the hopes of enlightened reform. But by 1779, when Houdon formally exhibited his *Franklin,* yet another, and final, stage in Franklin's iconography had been reached. By then his image had transcended mere representation and entered into allegory. The physical person— ideologized by Cochin and Nini and vividly realized by Caffiéri and Houdon—is left behind, transposed into a symbol within a realm of visual metaphors.

Franklin first appears in allegory in a casual sketch by Fragonard, dashed off in a single morning, early in 1778, to allow his friend, the amateur artist the Abbé de Saint-Non, to demonstrate to Franklin the new process of aquatint engraving. As finished by Saint-Non, the print [fig. 55] shows a warm, gentle scene, in which a pleasant-looking Liberty is about to crown with laurel leaves the Caffiéri bust of Franklin, which is held by an angel atop a terrestrial globe. Pennsylvania's constitution is draped across the globe, and the symbolic liberty cap and pole appear above, in beams of light.

Later in the year Fragonard turned more seriously to the same theme, and produced a striking print [fig. 56]. Franklin, in a voluminous toga, is seated aloft, and at his knee sits America, holding the nation's fasces. One of Franklin's arms points high above to a winged

Fig. 55: *Le Docteur Franklin Couronné par la Liberté*

Minerva fending off lightning with her shield; the other arm points below to a ferocious Mars cutting down Tyranny and Avarice with a savage backhanded cut of his sword. The integration of the design by the gesture of Franklin's arms, the flow and spontaneity of the arrangement of figures and drapery are the work of a master artist. And the message is clear. The print bears Turgot's famous epigram, suppressed by the censors in earlier representations but now officially approved: *Eripuit coelo fulmen, sceptrumque tirannis*—He seized lightning from the sky and the scepter from tyrants.

Fig. 56: *Eripuit Coelo Fulmen, Sceptrumque Tirannis*

Fragonard's skill stands out in contrast to the other major allegorical print of 1778, that of Antoine Borel [fig. 57]. Drawn independently of Fragonard's, it has similar elements: Franklin is again in Roman costume (though now sandaled and wreathed); one hand is on the shoulder of America (now a half-naked female Indian); a protective Minerva swirls above (now a spear thrower against evil);

Fig. 57: *L'Amérique Indépendante*

and Mars beats down Britain and Neptune with a backhanded smash of his club. But the ambitious Borel, hoping to find favor with American patrons, added much more to the scene. Now Prudence appears, close to Franklin's side; Liberty stands high on a pedestal holding the liberty cap and pole; Commerce, Agriculture, and the Arts are there, viewing with satisfaction the destruction of

Fig. 58

Fig. 59

Roger Sherman, by Ralph Earl (1775–76). A self-educated farmer, lawyer, jurist, and landowner, and a major figure in the Philadelphia Convention, he struck contemporaries as "unaccountably strange in his manner," his way of speaking "grotesque and laughable," yet "in his train of thinking there is something regular, deep and comprehensive."

Oliver Ellsworth and his wife, Abigail, by Ralph Earl (1792). Elegant provincials, they sit stiffly and proudly before their "seat" in Windsor, Connecticut, he holding a copy of the Constitution, which he helped draft, she, at age thirty-six the mother of nine children, in the formal dress of a well-to-do country gentlewoman.

The ultimate portrait of Franklin, in Paris, by Joseph Siffred Duplessis (1778). The frame, crowded with symbols, bears the simple but portentous legend *VIR*—man: Franklin as the embodiment of the Enlightenment's hopes for all mankind.

Fig. 60

Britain; three small, anonymous faces—of mankind?—press forward from a corner of the background to catch a glimpse of the
scene; and in the deeper background an exotic tree blossoms, a symbol of the New World context in which the action is placed. In all,
thirteen faces crowd Borel's print. It is as static as Fragonard's flow-
ing picture is dynamic, as pedantic as Fragonard's is artistic, as lit-
eral as Fragonard's is poetic. But, however different, both prints,
famous in their own time and after, show Franklin as a mythological
figure, the liberator of America and the nemesis of evil, tyranny,
and Britain.

But while Franklin thus entered the pantheon of mythological figures in the allegories of the time, his physical presence continued to
fascinate the artistic, fashionable, and ideological world, sometimes

Fig. 61

with odd results. Amédée Van Loo turned out a rather bemused, smiling, very private Franklin, painted for the personal enjoyment of Mme Helvétius [fig. 58]; later, during the French Revolution, it would be redone as a more pensive, puzzled figure by Pierre-Michel Alix [fig. 59]. The famous Jean-Baptiste Greuze painted a sly-looking Franklin half in shadows and most elegantly clothed [fig. 60]. Jacques Thouron, in a miniature enamel, projected a tight-lipped face with wildly windblown hair [fig. 61]. And Franklin's talented neighbor, the young, romantic Anne-Rosalie Filleul, produced a dashing figure, a man-about-town in a fur-trimmed dressing gown, shirt collar rakishly open, and a white satin waistcoat crossed over the chest in double-breasted fashion [fig. 62]. The engraving made from her painting bore not only the now standard Turgot epigram but the almost obligatory "*Né à Boston le 17 Janvier 1706*," a datum mocked by the subject's youthful appearance.

So, as the American delegation strove to fulfill its mission, the ideals, the goals, of the American cause became more and more

BENJAMIN FRANKLIN

*Né a Boston le 17 Janvier 1706.*

Eripuit coelo fulmen sceptrum que tyrannis.

Fig. 62

focused on the image of Franklin, now fused with the aspirations of the Enlightenment itself. But then, in 1778, one final painting, the masterpiece of Franklin portraiture, took all of this visual commentary to an ultimate step—beyond allegory and the symbols of virtue and vice—and identified Franklin with humanity itself, its achievements, hopes, and possibilities.

No one who viewed the "fur collar" portrait by Joseph Siffred Duplessis [fig. 63; see also color insert], the leading royal portraitist, when it was first exhibited in 1779 doubted that this was a supreme artistic achievement. The rhapsodies that greeted the work, commissioned by the same Le Ray de Chaumont who had sponsored the Nini medallion and who continued to host the American representatives in Passy, cannot, in retrospect, be thought excessive. The explicit messages and the ideological gadgetry of the earlier portraits are left behind. The face is worn, the skin pouched, the eyes somewhat puffed and tired, but the portrait radiates experience, wisdom, patience, tolerance, and a world-weariness beyond all cleverness and guile. Yet the firm, pursed lips are resolute and purposeful, and the faint smile engaging. One sees, and feels, a dignified presence, a calm, dispassionate, rich personality unconstrained by nationality, occupation, or rank. The frame, ornate and gilded, is crowded with symbols—rattlesnake, liberty cap, and lion's-skin trophy beneath an elevated wreath of triumph—but the picture itself is uncluttered, and the simple, powerfully understated legend, not "Franklin" but "*Vir*"—man or mankind—conveys, as nothing more elaborate could have done, the elemental quality that Duplessis had seized.[18] Franklin knew that this was the ultimate visual depiction of his life, and so he declined, in the years that followed, to sit for further portraits, telling ambitious artists simply to copy Duplessis, which they, and Duplessis himself, did again and again, until this portrait of the triumphant year 1778 became a timeless icon of Enlightenment hopes and America's role in human history.

At Franklin's death, twelve years later, Duplessis's "*Vir*" would reappear, as the legend on a memorial bust of the "illustre philantrope" placed dramatically at the center of a black-draped room

Fig. 63

Fig. 64: *L'Apotre de la Liberté Immortalisé*

by Les Amis de la Révolution et de l'Humanité.[19] It was one among
many memorials, *éloges*, and obsequies devoted to Franklin's memory
in France, among them a final pair of allegories, now of his celestial
elevation. At first [fig. 64] he is shown drawn rather uncomfortably
between Immortality, cradling his head and lifting him up into the
bosom of divinity, while Death, clinging to his leg, attempts to drag
him into the fires of Oblivion. America, nude, kneels at his side amid
broken shackles; France and Philosophy weep at his demise; his
fame is trumpeted to the universe; and a lightning rod draws fire
from the sky. But once safely aloft [fig. 65], he is in charge in the
Champs-Elysées, welcoming Mirabeau to the company of Rousseau, Montesquieu, Voltaire, Mably, and Fénelon, whose main writings are well displayed, while Demosthenes and Cicero look on in
admiration.

But portraiture, statuary, and allegorical engravings did not

Fig. 65: *Mirabeau Arrive aux Champs Élisées*

exhaust the symbolism of Franklin's presence in Paris. Pageantry was equally important. The year of triumph, 1778, was as famous for its political theatre as it was for its artistic achievements, and in this realm nothing exceeded the great public spectacles of Franklin's meetings with Voltaire.

In February 1778 Voltaire had returned to Paris after years of exile. Upon his arrival Franklin took the whole American delegation, including his grandson, Temple, to visit the old man (he was eighty-four, Franklin seventy-two). And then, in a great assemblage of people, he asked Voltaire to bless his grandson as a symbol of mankind's future. Voltaire complied, uttering the benediction "God and Liberty!" Whereupon, Voltaire reported, everyone wept.[20]

Two months later Voltaire was initiated into the Masonic order, entering the Lodge of the Nine Sisters on Franklin's arm. And finally, on April 29, the greatest scene of all took place, which Adams, to his intense mortification, was obliged to witness. "After dinner," Adams later recorded in his autobiography,

> we went to the Academy of Sciences, and heard Mr. D'Alembert as Secretary perpetual, pronounce eulogies on several of their members lately deceased. Voltaire and Franklin were both present, and there presently arose a general cry that Monsieur Voltaire and Monsieur Franklin should be introduced to each other. This was done and they bowed and spoke to each other. This was no satisfaction. There must be something more. Neither of our philosophers seemed to divine what was wished or expected. They however took each other by the hand . . . But this was not enough. The clamour continued, untill the explanation came out "Il faut s'embrasser, à la françoise." The two aged actors upon this great theatre of philosophy and frivolity then embraced each other by hugging one another in their arms and kissing each others cheeks, and then the tumult subsided. And the cry immediately spread through the whole Kingdom and I suppose over all Europe Qu'il etoit charmant. Oh! il etoit enchantant . . . to see Solon and Sophocles embracing![21]

Is it not true that America's successes, its great historical moments, have occurred when idealism and realism were combined? Three months earlier, the life-saving Franco-American alliance, largely negotiated by Franklin, had been concluded. It was secured not by one treaty but by two: the first a treaty of amity and commerce that conformed to the ideals of the model treaty; the second a secret pact—pure power politics—by which France guaranteed American independence and gave the new nation the right to conquer Canada in exchange for France's right to seize the British West Indies; both sides pledged not to conclude peace with Britain without the other's consent.[22] By June France was at war with Britain, and the configuration of Atlantic power politics was transformed. The question thereafter was not *if* America would win the War of Independence, but *when.*

The blending of realism and idealism permeates the entire history of the Revolutionary era. The climax—and perhaps the most vivid example of Gilbert's argument—came a decade after Adams arrived in Paris and a decade after the most creative phase of Franklin's iconography, in the drafting, ratification, and amending of the federal Constitution.

For many years it has been fashionable to view the Constitution as the conservative reversal of the idealism of the early years of the Revolution—a counterrevolution, a Thermidor. But it was not. It was much more complicated, much more subtle, than that. The Constitution was written not by hard-nosed, conservative political bosses determined to reverse the meliorist enthusiasm of the early years, but by idealists, tempered idealists, who had come to recognize, reluctantly, the need to create the dangerous instruments of centralized power.[23] Survival, they realized—economic, political, military—depended on it. But they knew the dangers. They had fought a war to escape the controls of a powerful imperial government that could impose military rule at will, destroy civil liberties, and impoverish the population by taxation. The possibility that the independent government they were creating might reproduce precisely the same dangers was never far from their minds, and in the ratification debate the powerful opposition was there to remind the Federalists of the dangers of excessive executive power, autocratic majoritarianism, military adventurism, the loss of civil liberties, and the emergence of oligarchic or aristocratic domination. It was to eliminate or closely control those dangers while creating an effective national government that the Federalists devised their complex tissue of compromises, balances, checks and cross-checks that make up the federal Constitution. So the empowering Section 8 of Article I enumerates in eighteen paragraphs the central powers of the national government, but the eight paragraphs of Section 9 that immediately follow lay down restrictions on precisely the powers enumerated. So the president proposes, but Congress disposes. So armies are created, but financed by civilians, biennially. So the president devises treaties, but the Senate enacts them. So the executive nominates judges, but the Senate confirms them. Every sentence was parsed, weighed, challenged. Some wondered whether such an intricately balanced machine could ever work.

But still it was not enough. The purpose of it all was to secure the needs, the rights, of the people. Why was there no Bill of Rights? Good, logical, apparently irrefutable answers were given by the Federalist leaders. First, the government *could* not invade areas of personal rights, since its mandate extended only to specified and limited powers; second, most states already had bills of rights, and it was at the state level that such matters should be handled; third, if you enumerate rights, you limit their plentitude to the few items you happened to think of; and fourth, "parchment barriers," as Madison put it, a few luminous words on paper, would not keep ambitious men from exercising undue power: freedom can be preserved not by glowing statements but by the balance of real forces.

Good arguments, but the opposition was unconvinced. They saw a deeper logic. If rights were not specified in some form but were simply assumed to exist, in the end someone in government would have to say, in a contested situation, what precisely the rights were that should be legally protected, and so those who held office could silence opposition simply by refusing to recognize rights that were claimed. In the end—after one of the most exhaustive public debates in modern history—the message was clear: there would be no Constitution unless the corpus of powers that had been created were balanced by an equally powerful enumeration of rights; unless it were explicitly stated that all powers not specifically delegated to the federal government were reserved to the people or to the states; and unless the enumerated rights were understood not to deny or disparage or limit all other rights, whatever they were, which were reserved in their totality to the people.[24]

Like the Franco-American alliance of 1778, the Constitution is not a singular document; it is two documents, one creating the powers necessary for survival, the other expressing enlightened aspirations. It is a bill of powers and a bill of rights combined, and in its amended, complete form it reflects precisely the creative tension between idealism and realism in American public life that Felix Gilbert saw so clearly in his earliest studies in America. His conclusion, that America's "great historical moments have occurred when both were combined"—the perception of a mind shaped by harsh Prussian realities and studies of Renaissance politics, sensitively responding to North American ideals—is as true today as it was when he wrote it, over forty years ago.

# IV

## The *Federalist* Papers

Generations of people—scholars and politicians alike—have believed the *Federalist* papers to be the finest explanation of the principles that underlie the American government and the most accurate analysis of the intentions of those who designed it. More than that, the *Federalist* papers seem to many to have a timeless, transhistorical quality. The New York jurist Chancellor Kent concluded that they were superior to any work on the principles of free government, and that, he said, included the works of Aristotle, Cicero, Machiavelli, Montesquieu, Milton, Locke, and Burke. It is still, Benjamin Wright, a distinguished modern authority on the subject, wrote, "by far the greatest book on politics ever written in America"—written, that is, on politics as such, not merely on our own national brand of politics.

Informed Europeans agreed. When the Spanish ambassador to France confessed to Talleyrand that he did not know *The Federalist,* the foreign minister wasted no sympathy on him: "Then read it," he told the envoy curtly, "read it." Later, Guizot said *The Federalist* "was the greatest work known to him" in applying the principles of government to practical administration. And in England, a writer in *Blackwood's Magazine,* echoing views in the *Edinburgh Review,* wrote that *The Federalist* may be called, "seriously, reverently, the Bible of Republicanism . . . which for comprehensiveness of design, strength, clearness, and simplicity has no parallel" even in the works of Montesquieu and Aristotle.[1]

But the *Federalist* papers were not always thought of as such a profound document, especially by the small number of the authors' contemporaries who are known to have read the papers as they appeared. The Antifederalists, of course, who were determined to prevent the adoption of the Constitution as it had been submitted, challenged the *Federalist* papers' arguments when they did not simply dismiss them out of hand—as one Antifederalist did who said *The Federalist* would "jade the brain of any poor sinner" and another did by claiming that *The Federalist* had mistaken "sound for argument . . . accumulated myriads of unmeaning sentences, and *mechanically* endeavored to force conviction by a torrent of misplaced words." And while many of the Federalists praised the papers, some of them too had doubts. Washington's former secretary, for example, the Federalist judge A. C. Hanson, conceded that the papers were penetrating in part and "ingenious," but he confessed that he found them sophistical in some places, obvious in others, and throughout simply tiresome: they do not "force the attention," he wrote, "rouze the passions, or thrill the nerves."[2]

The paradoxes multiply the closer one looks. The papers are assumed to have been a collaborative effort by Alexander Hamilton, James Madison, and John Jay; but in fact the authors worked quite independently. Madison and Hamilton began but then quickly stopped reviewing each other's papers before they were published, and there is no evidence that one writer's work was ever revised on the advice of either of the others. While there was broad agreement on fundamental points and an acknowledgment of each author's particular concerns, there was no "special allotment," Madison wrote, "of the different parts of the subject to the several writers" and no concurrence on the weight to be given the various issues. "Frequently one half of 'Publius' [Hamilton or Madison] would not know what the other half said until he read the article in the newspaper." At one point, Madison and Hamilton appeared to disagree so strongly that John Quincy Adams said they were writing what he called "rival dissertations." One modern historian has diagnosed the papers as suffering from "a split personality," others have said its trouble is intellectual "schizophrenia." Madison himself admitted that the authors had distinct differences "in the general complexion of their political theories," and had no desire "to give a positive sanction to all the doctrines and sentiments of the other[s]." None of the writers were "mutually answerable for all the ideas of each other." Some later commentators have concluded that the papers are simply a work of political rhetoric written to gloss over the compromises of the Constitution and to make that document look consistent; still others have claimed that in terms of systematic political theory the papers are trivial. However that may be (and we shall return to that) there is no doubt that the authors had different kinds of commitments to the project. Of the eighty-five papers, John Jay wrote only five; Madison, twenty-nine; Hamilton, fifty-one. Hamilton was the manager of the project throughout. It was he who proposed the series in the first place, and it was he who published the first thirty-six papers together as volume I of the book edition and who added eight new papers of his own to those that had appeared in newspapers to round out the second volume.[3]

There was something helter-skelter about the whole enterprise: there are "violations of method," Hamilton confessed in the preface to the book edition, "and repetitions of ideas which cannot but displease a critical reader." Which is hardly surprising, in view of the circumstances. Hamilton wrote the first number on board a river sloop traveling from Albany to Manhattan. The seventy-seven papers that were first published in newspapers appeared twice a week, then four times a week, and so had to be written at great speed. Some were simply dashed off to meet the printers' deadlines. Madison later wrote that often "whilst the printer was putting into type parts of a number, the following parts were under the pen and to be furnished in time for the press." During the most intense period of the work, Madison, an active member of the Continental Congress then meeting in New York, and Hamilton, busy in his law practice, were both writing an essay every three or four days. In six months the authors wrote and published an average of 1,000 words a day; between October 1787 and May 1788 Hamilton and Madison wrote for publication 175,000 words. In their haste they understandably and necessarily drew on—at times copied—things they had written before. Without this prepared material, Madison later confessed, the papers could not have been written in time to be effective. Much of the most famous of the papers, No. 10, by Madison, was largely taken from a letter he had written to Jefferson a month earlier and from his "Vices of the Political System" written seven months before that. Three other papers by Madison (Nos. 18–20) were largely lifted from the reading notes on ancient and modern confederacies he had made a year before in preparation for the Constitutional Convention. Similarly, Hamilton took much of the design and some of the substance of his early contributions to the series from an elaborate speech he had delivered at the Philadelphia Convention. And some of the individual papers are not essays in themselves but sections of extended discourses broken off for the convenience of semiweekly newspaper publication. A block of twenty-one consecutive *Federalist* papers (Nos. 37–58) that Madison published over five weeks when Hamilton was attending the New York Supreme Court session (over 150 pages in the modern book editions) are simply sequential segments of a single, long, well-structured essay. Newspaper readers would have had to have collected the pieces as they appeared and to have saved them in order to read them together as the coherent unit they are.[4]

Far from an integrated, systematic treatise on basic principles of political theory produced in calm contemplation, the *Federalist* papers were polemical essays directed to specific institutional proposals written in the heat of a fierce political battle which every informed person knew would determine the future of the new nation. Yet generations of scholars, students, lawyers, and judges have approached the *Federalist* papers as if they were a formal, carefully deliberated discourse of basic theory. Every phrase in the *Federalist* papers has been studied by scholars for its possible meanings, and the Supreme Court, in decisions that affect the lives of all Americans, has increas-

ingly accepted the papers as a uniquely reliable source for the meaning of the Constitution. In the 210 years between the Court's first session and January 2000, there are records of 291 citations in the
Court's opinions: 1 in the eighteenth century, 58 in the nineteenth
century, 38 in the first half of the twentieth century, and no less than
194 in the second half. Analysis of the citations shows their uses by
both liberal and conservative justices and litigants on a remarkably
broad range of issues, from banking and taxation to the prohibition
of alcohol, from term limits to piracy, and from slavery to presidential election laws. At times the justices have considered the papers
important enough to challenge each other's interpretations of particular passages in them in the course of their written opinions.[5] There
is now a concordance of *The Federalist*—something one usually asso-
ciates with the Bible and the works of Shakespeare—in which every
use of every word in the eighty-five essays except articles, pronouns,
and the verb "to be" is listed out, together with the words that pre-
cede and follow it, to enable students to grasp through verbal context
every nuance that might be found in what these three very busy
politicians wrote.

In this near-religious veneration for a series of political arguments
that emerged from a frantic public struggle there is a strange and
important paradox. *The Federalist* is an eighteenth-century document, written in and limited by the circumstances of that distant
time; yet it is seen now, and increasingly, as not merely relevant in
some vague way to our postindustrial world but instructive, even pre-
scriptive, on specific problems of the twenty-first century. But the
authors of the *Federalist* papers lived in a preindustrial world whose
social and economic problems were utterly different from ours and
whose social policies, insofar as they had any, if implemented now
would create chaos. They knew about special interests and about
social and political passions, but they had no idea how powerfully
public opinion in a modern democracy can be manipulated, especially by instruments of communication they could not have conceived of. Much of their thinking—certainly Madison's—was based
on assumptions about physical distance and its calming and dissipat-

ing effect on political passions; but we live at a time when distance is obliterated and scattered forces can coalesce by instantaneous communication with intensifying effect. The instruments of coercive force that they knew, the machinery of physical intimidation, were far weaker than ours, and the modes of escaping from the power of the state more numerous.

Beyond all that, the Constitution that the *Federalist* papers defended and explained is simply a different instrument from the Constitution as we know it now. Hundreds of federal court decisions, in implementing clauses of the Constitution, have given them new shape. The amendments that have been added to the Constitution—especially the Civil War amendments which made possible the extension of the federal Bill of Rights into the states and overthrew the Founders' notions of citizenship—have fundamentally altered the scope and meaning of the Constitution. Further, the *Federalist* authors deplored political parties, which they identified not with broad policy positions but with narrow, selfish "factional" interests; but we know that, while special interests exist in abundance, political parties, for all their divisiveness, are essential to the functioning both of our federal system and of the separated powers within the federal and state governments. And the Founders made elaborate provision for what they called a filtration of popular influences which—in the form of electors specially chosen to select the president and state legislatures as electors of senators—we have discarded. It is a reworked, significantly amended Constitution that we live with. Yet, though modern commentators explain our present, elaborated Constitution as it now actually operates, we still go back to the *Federalist* papers, written more than two centuries ago, for instruction and understanding.

Why? Should we? What, if anything, accounts for *The Federalist*'s authority? Where does its value now lie?

The starting point, I believe, for understanding the relevance of *The Federalist* in our time is to go back to the context from which the papers emerged.

In 1878 William Gladstone, the British prime minister, declared that the American Constitution was "the most wonderful work ever struck off at a given time by the brain and purpose of man."[6] He was right about the wonder of the Constitution, but he was wrong about the "given time." It was no product of a single stroke. The creation of the Constitution stretched out through four distinct stages: from 1787 at least to the end of Washington's first administration in 1793.

The first stage was, of course, the secret constitutional convention in Philadelphia in which the Constitution was written—May to September 1787. Only fifty-five people attended that four-month convention, but in itself it was an extended process—a history in itself—of subtle and complex changes, compromises, revisions, and adjustments.

The second stage was the public debate within the states on the ratification of the proposed Constitution, which lasted from late September 1787 through July 1788, when all the states but North Carolina and Rhode Island ratified. It was understood at least halfway through that process that amendments, based on proposals from the states, would be added that would constitute a Bill of Rights.

The third stage was the work of the first session of the First Congress, March to September 1789, when two fundamental supplements to the Constitution were made. In the House, the first ten amendments, the Bill of Rights, were devised, by Madison working with some eighty of the states' recommendations, and sent out to the states for approval. In the Senate, the Judiciary Act, drafted by Oliver Ellsworth, was passed, which fleshed out the Constitution's brief Article III, on the judiciary, by creating the federal court system and giving to it powers that the people in Philadelphia had not dared to include.

But still, the whole thing was merely words on paper until implemented by Washington's government. Washington knew how malleable the situation was; he understood that every move he and his administration made would be a precedent that would shape the actuality of the Constitution, and he proceeded with great care. It was Washington, for example, who created the structure of the executive offices (the cabinet) and it was he who defined the Senate's role in foreign policy and something of the operational meaning of the words "advice and consent."

In this long and complicated process, the ratification debates—the second stage—have a peculiar importance, and provide the immediate context for understanding the *Federalist* papers.

The initial publication of the Constitution on September 19, 1787, and Congress's call for the states to vote on ratification touched off one of the most extensive public debates on constitutionalism and on political principles ever recorded.[7] The entire political nation was galvanized in the debate. Literally thousands of people, in this nation of only approximately one million eligible voters, participated in one way or another. There were some fifteen hundred official delegates to the twelve state ratifying conventions, where every section, every clause and every phrase of the Constitution was raked over. There was a multitude of newspaper commentaries, sermons, letters, broadsides, and personal debates on the Constitution; they turned up in even the most remote corners of the nation. The *Federalist* papers were not the only extended series of essays published during the months of ratification. There were in fact twenty-four such series besides *The Federalist*, some of which, like the sixteen papers written in New York under the pseudonym "Brutus," were perceptive and penetrating, and were responded to, not always successfully, by Madison and especially by Hamilton. At the very end of the entire project Hamilton was still replying to "Brutus"'s fear that the Supreme Court justices would "feel themselves independent of Heaven itself."[8]

Not all the critical papers were as intelligent as "Brutus"'s. There were blasts of verbal violence, like those that erupted in a series in Philadelphia that called the supporters of the Constitution the "meanest traitors that ever dishonoured the human character," and accused them of conspiring to create "one *despotic monarchy* in America," concluding that "the days of a cruel Nero approach fast." But most of the writings and speeches in this great debate—in which alone, Madison later wrote, could be found the true meaning of the

Constitution—were sensible, and through them all there was one dominant theme: *fear*.[9]

Everyone involved in the controversy knew what the central issue was. The American Revolution in its essence had been a struggle against unconstrained centralized power—not power in some raw, unmediated sense, but power as it was understood within the ideological context of British political thought in which the Founders were immersed and which they themselves helped develop. This understanding, this set of mind, was a complex universe of attitudes, memories, beliefs, and aspirations whose roots go back to classical antiquity, the Renaissance, and the English civil war of the seventeenth century and which matured in the reformist theories of early-eighteenth-century Britain. It was in effect a map full of danger markers and historic signposts to guide one to political safety. Events of the 1760s and 1770s had been seen by the politically aware to be the signs of an approaching autocracy, to which the reasonable and necessary response was resistance, in the end rebellion. The result had been the deliberate resistance to and then the destruction of a centralized power system—a rebellion against British power justified, not by the egalitarian aspirations of the masses (most of the Revolution's leaders were socially conservative), but by the belief that unconstrained power will destroy free states, which are fragile, and the liberties that free people enjoy.[10]

Impelled by the threat they felt as they interpreted developing events within this complex of beliefs, the Revolutionaries, after destroying the British power system, had put their faith in the smaller, weaker, local governments of the states, linked together into a loose national confederation that was more a consultative body than a functioning government with the powers associated with national states. But with the proposed Constitution, in 1787, the movement of the Revolution seemed to have been reversed. The proposal before the ratifying conventions was not the dissolution of power but the opposite: the rebuilding of a potentially powerful central government that would have armed force, that would enter into all the dangerous struggles of international conflicts, and that had the potential to sweep through the states and dominate the daily lives of the American people.

So fear and the responses to fear dominated the debate on ratification—fear of recreating a dangerous central power system, similar, it seemed, to what they had only recently escaped from. For some, fear was unbounded. In North Carolina it was ominously observed that there was nothing in the Constitution that would prevent the pope from becoming president—a charge that James Iredell, the future Supreme Court justice and the author of a brilliant five-part essay series in favor of ratification, deemed worthy of refutation:

> No man but a native, and who has resided fourteen years in America, can be chosen President. I know not all the qualifications for a Pope, but I believe he must be taken from the College of Cardinals . . . A native of America must have very singular good fortune, who after residing fourteen years in his own country, should go to Europe, enter into Romish orders, obtain the promotion of Cardinal, afterwards that of Pope, and at length be so much in the confidence of his own country, as to be elected President. It would be still more extraordinary if he should give up his Popedom for our Presidency.[11]

But most of the fears were directed not to what the Constitution failed to prohibit but what it proposed specifically to enact.

In examining the provisions of the document, the critics had at times an eerie prescience. Some pointed to the supremacy clause in Article VI, which states that the Constitution and federal laws and treaties "shall be the supreme law of the land; and the judges in every state shall be bound thereby, anything in the Constitution or laws of any state to the contrary notwithstanding." Surely, it was argued, the supremacy clause made the whole idea of federalism a farce. The nation's laws, the Antifederalists said, would inevitably penetrate into the states and override state laws and state court decisions.

Many of the critics concentrated on the federal taxing power. The power to tax, "Brutus" wrote, exercised without limitation, will introduce itself into every corner of the city and country. It [the national government] will wait upon the ladies at their toilett, and will not leave them in any of their domestic concerns; it will accompany them to the ball, the play, and the assembly . . . it will enter the house of every gentleman, watch over his cellar, wait upon his cook in the kitchen, follow the servants into the parlour, preside over the table, and note down all he eats and drinks; it will attend him to his bedchamber and watch him while he sleeps; it will take cognizance of the professional man in his office, or his study . . . it will follow the mechanic to his shop, and in his work, and will haunt him in his family, and in his bed . . . it will penetrate into the most obscure cottage; and finally, it will light upon the head of every person in the United States. To all these different classes of people, and in all these circumstances in which it will attend them, the language in which it will address them will be, GIVE! GIVE!

They feared the treaty-making power—some because they thought the president should not have the power to negotiate agreements in secret, others because they feared that a president who could command a bare two-thirds majority in the Senate would be able to commit the country to anything he wished, whether millions of ordinary citizens liked it or not. But the Senate's power was feared for more reasons than that. It was feared because its members' six-year tenure seemed "aristocratical"; it was feared for its power to block presidential appointments, which might lead—who knew?—to political deal making; and it was feared too for its role as a court of impeachment. Was it not possible, one Antifederalist asked, that a president might someday use hidden slush funds, just as the British had done, to enable the "secret services" to engage in covert operations in defiance of the people's representatives, and then, through the pardoning power, "screen from punishment those whom he had secretly instigated to commit the crime, and thereby prevent a discovery of his own guilt"? The president could of course be impeached—but the impeachment trial court would be the Senate, a group he might well dominate, and in any case, it was noted, the trial would be presided over by a chief justice whom the president himself

had nominated, and nominated "probably not so much for his eminence in legal knowledge and for his integrity, as from favouritism
and [political] influence . . . a person of whose voice and influence
he shall consider himself secure." A fantastic, unreal scenario? Some
in 1788 did not think so.[12]

Dangers, for some, appeared wherever one looked—in every turn
of phrase and possible implication of the Constitution.

A national, professional army? But they had only recently overcome Britain's "standing army" and they knew from history how
standing armies could become bloodthirsty palace guards, janis-
saries, to be manipulated against the people by an overambitious
executive. And what kind of a protection would there be from the
states' militias, since, according to the Constitution, they could be
nationalized by the same ambitious president on the excuse of some
possible threat from abroad?

A federal district was proposed for the seat of the national government. But an area where the people had no representation and
where Congress would rule directly, uninhibited by an intervening
state government—was *that* a good idea? "Few clauses in the Constitution," George Mason, the author of the first state bill of rights,
declared, were as dangerous as this. The federal district, he said,
would become "the sanctuary of the blackest crimes." The place,
Patrick Henry added, might well become the headquarters of a powerful army controlled solely by Congress. "Is there any act," he
asked, "however atrocious which [Congress] cannot do by virtue of
this clause? Can you say that you will be safe when you give [Con-
gress] such unlimited powers, without any real responsibility? . . .
Will not the Members of Congress have the same passions which
other rulers have had? They will not be superior to the frailties of
human nature." A district that has no representation in the government that rules them, a judge in Virginia's Kentucky district wrote,
"will be the most successful nursery of slaves that ever was devised by
man." It will be a market where honors and emoluments bestowed
by the government will be sufficient to buy the liberty and with it the
loyalty of "the bulk of mankind . . . these numerous and wealthy

slaves will infallibly be devoted to the views of their masters; and having surrendered their own will always be ready to trample on the rights of free men."

"Brutus" saw a subtler, more insidious danger—in the federal government's power to "borrow money on the credit of the United States." With this power, he wrote, Congress "may create a national debt, so large as to exceed the ability of the country ever to sink. I can scarcely contemplate a greater calamity that could befal[l] this country than to be loaded with a debt exceeding their ability ever to discharge . . . it is unwise and improvident to vest in the general government a power to borrow at discretion, without any limitation or restriction." Given all these dangers and many more, the Antifederalists were shocked to discover that the Constitution, unlike most state constitutions, did not include a Bill of Rights to protect people against the threatening powers of the government being created. On this flagrant omission they attacked the Federalists again and again.[13]

Such were the Antifederalists' arguments, worked out in elaborate critiques of almost every clause of the Constitution, which Hamilton, Madison, and Jay undertook to refute in the *Federalist* papers. The task was peculiarly difficult not simply because the arguments against the Constitution were for the most part cogent and well informed but because these objections had behind them the authority of a sanctified tradition. They were drawn—often literally—from the ideas, ideals, and fears that had led to the rebellion against Britain, and these were fears and beliefs and ideals not of the passing moment but fundamental to the deepest values of Anglo-American political culture. They were embedded in the world view, the ideological complex, that had dominated Americans' political understanding just a short decade earlier and that had impelled the rebellion against Britain.

The great achievement of the authors of the *Federalist* papers is not merely that they replied in detail to specific dangers that critics saw in the Constitution and explained in detail how the new govern-

ment should, and would, work, but that they did so without repudi-
ating the past, without rejecting the basic ideology of the Revolution.
Indeed, their ultimate accomplishment was to remove the Revolutionary ideology from what Hamilton called "halcyon scenes of the
poetic or fabulous age" and place it squarely in the real world with all
"the vicissitudes and calamities which have fallen to the lot of other
nations." *The Federalist* sought to embrace the Revolutionary heritage, and then to update it in ways that would make it consistent
with the inescapable necessity of creating an effective national
power.[14]

The Constitution, in creating a strong central government, *The
Federalist* argued, did not betray the Revolution, with its radical hopes
for greater political freedom than had been known before. Quite the
contrary, it fulfilled those radical aspirations, by creating the power
necessary to guarantee both the nation's survival and the preservation of the people's and the states' rights.

Soberly, patiently, sometimes repetitiously, *The Federalist* took up,
analyzed, and responded to all the major issues. It was difficult,
uphill work—difficult intellectually, politically, even psychologi-
cally—and there was no predictable outcome. They knew that the
political world they were trying to create, uniting national power and
personal liberty, was something new under the sun, and that the
mere contemplation of such an unknown world stimulated morbid,
malignant fantasies of impending doom—"frightful and distorted
shapes—gorgons, hydras, and chimeras dire," "palpable illusion[s]
of the imagination"—that could frustrate all their realistic arguments. But confident themselves of a future based on the new Constitution, they sought to overcome these amorphous, free-floating
anxieties and keep the struggle within realistic bounds. No doubt, as
one debater in the North Carolina ratifying convention put it, "those
things which *can* be, *may* be," but if every omission in the Constitution is magnified into "a plot against the national rights," Madison
wrote, no improvement in the state of the nation would ever be
accomplished. "Where in the name of common sense," Hamilton
said, "are our fears to end if we may not trust our sons, our brothers,

our neighbours, our fellow-citizens? What shadow of danger can there be from men who are daily mingling with the rest of their countrymen, and who participate with them in the same feelings, sentiments, habits and interests?"[15]

So while attempting to calm the dark, unfocused fears that permeated the political atmosphere, *The Federalist* took up the real, palpable threats posed by an enlarged and effective central government.

Would not the federal government overwhelm the states, take over their powers, supersede their laws, and sacrifice their local needs to some abstract "general interest" that would be to no one's benefit but those who controlled the central power? To this *The Federalist* replied: how *could* it? The federal government was designed as a creation of the states; it would depend on the states for its existence, while the states would continue to exist independently of the nation. The states would enact the procedures for presidential elections, they would elect the senators, they would probably collect some of the federal taxes, and they would retain all the rights and powers not specifically delegated to the federal government. The powers assigned the federal government are "few and defined," the states' powers "numerous and indefinite . . . extend[ing] to all the objects which, in the ordinary course of affairs, concern the life, liberties, and properties of the people." And in any case, people are always more attached to, more loyal to, their local, familiar institutions than to a distant, unseen power; and local, state attachments will determine the actions of the people's representatives in Congress. The two governments, state and national, would not be adversaries. They would have different powers, of different magnitudes, to serve different purposes, which would only occasionally overlap. If, by some turn of events, the federal government did manage to encroach on, assault, the powers of the states, the people in the states would defeat it by refusing to cooperate and by joining together to create procedural roadblocks. And if, beyond even that, it ever came to some kind of military confrontation, the official state militias equipped with their own arms (as the Second Amendment, anticipated by Hamilton, would later guarantee) would overwhelm any "standing army" that the executive could create.[16]

But what would prevent the executive from building up an oppressive army, a "standing army," to overwhelm the liberties of the people? To this profound fear, based on the whole heritage of ancient and modern history, Hamilton, for whom the creation of a national army was a major concern, devoted some of his most closely wrought papers. So long as the Constitution functioned, he wrote—that is, so long as there was no complete overthrow of all civil institutions by a coup d'état—a military buildup, under the rules of the Constitution, would require "progressive augmentations" of Congressional appropriations, and since military appropriations had to be renewed every two years, that would happen only if there were a conspiracy between Congress and the president sustained over successive transformations of House membership. Was it even remotely conceivable, Hamilton asked, that every incoming congressman would instantly "commence a traitor to his constituents and to his country"? And if there ever were such a fantastic plot, how could it be concealed?[17]

But if the states and the nation were not likely to clash in arms, would they not come into conflict in other ways since in some areas they had what seemed to be overlapping jurisdictions? Everyone knew that two or more sovereign governments could not coexist in the same territory: sovereignty in its nature was absolute and exclusive. That famous doctrine had in fact lain at the root of the conflict with Britain; if those two powers, Parliament and the colonial governments, both of which claimed sovereignty, the one explicitly, the other implicitly, could have existed together cooperatively there would have been no revolution. What difference, it was asked, was there between the Constitution's "supremacy clause" and Britain's Declaratory Act, which had declared Parliament to have "full power . . . to bind . . . the people of America . . . in all cases whatsoever"? To this, *The Federalist* replied that while the ancient doctrine that dual sovereignties could not coexist was undeniable and had correctly applied in the pre-Revolutionary situation, it did not apply in the present case since neither of the governments was a sovereign entity. They were both agencies of the one and only absolute sovereign power, the people, and the people could appoint any combination of governmental agencies they chose to serve their purposes.[18]

But were there not other fatal flaws in the structure of the system? Might not the federal government, as "Brutus" feared, empowered as it was to "lay and collect taxes," impoverish the nation by endless taxation? For Hamilton, this was a fiscal and administrative question, for Madison a matter of verbal precision. Federal taxation, Hamilton wrote, would be either indirect (tariffs and excises) or direct (taxes on property or polls). If indirect, consumers would defeat excessive taxation by cutting down on the consumption of the targeted goods and so defeat the effort. If direct, first, the modest means of the majority of farmers would yield too little from taxes on land and houses; second, personal property other than real estate is "too precarious and invisible a fund" to tax properly; and third, poll taxes are so universally obnoxious that no sensible government would resort to them except in dire emergencies.[19]

Madison replied to the fears of federal taxation by turning to the wording of the empowering clause in Article I, Section 8. One finds there, he said, no limitless authorization to tax. Yes, Congress is empowered to lay and collect taxes—that was one of the main reasons for writing the Constitution—but only "to pay the debts and provide for the common defense and general welfare of the United States." And as for the phrase "general welfare," it is no open-ended license to prey on the community. It is specifically explained and qualified, Madison wrote, by the enumerated particulars in the clauses that immediately follow. Shall these "clear and precise expressions," Madison asked, "be denied any signification" and only "the more doubtful and indefinite terms be retained in their full extent"? That, he said, would be absurd.[20]

The real question, Madison and Hamilton both concluded, is not whether federal taxation would impoverish the nation but whether the natural bias against any and all taxation, the difficulty of collecting federal taxes, and the competing financial needs of the states would not prevent the general government from ever raising the funds it needed to do its work.

But financially oppressive or not, how could such a continental-sized government actually work? How could the myriad interests in such a nation—at its birth five times the size of Britain, and likely to grow—how could such an immense nation possibly be represented in a single legislature of manageable size? Would not the great diversity of factions, private ambitions, and passionate causes, all of them entirely free to flourish in any way they could, lead to a chaotic struggle of all against all? Would not the sheer size of the country make it impossible to achieve the consensus needed to sustain the government?

To this fundamental question *The Federalist* replied calmly, cogently, clearly, and concisely. Direct representation of the innumerable interests of the people, many of them passionate and extreme in their partisan ambitions, was neither desirable nor possible; it was, Hamilton wrote, "altogether visionary." The combination of large electoral districts and a relatively small House of Representatives would necessarily lead to the selection of moderate representatives agreeable to many factions and cross-sections of the population. Further, the institutional complexity of the national government would tend to neutralize conflicts among factions as they attempted to work through the government, and draw them together into moderated coalitions. But beyond all of that, the system would lead to the selection as representatives those who would be likely to stand above special interests and pursue the true interests of all their constituents, as well as the common good of society. Thus, Hamilton wrote, mechanics and tradesmen would have mutual interests in selecting merchants, their natural patrons and economic allies, to represent them, and these would be men of "influence and weight and superior acquirements." For landholders, rich and poor, "middling farmers," "moderate proprietors of land," would be the natural, sensible representatives. And above all, members of the learned professions, especially lawyers, "who truly form no distinct interest in society," were likely to be "the objects of the confidence and choice of each other and of other parts of the country." The goal of representation, Hamilton wrote, was not to mirror the infinity of private interests in the way a pure democracy would do, but to meld the contesting forces into the permanent and collective interests of the nation. The proper representatives, he wrote, were not those who understood only their home districts' local interests but those who, while informed and respectful of their constituents' "dispositions and inclinations," could grasp the technical issues of public policy and the logic of the nation's welfare, which in the end would benefit all. For this, the best-qualified people—in terms of education, independence, judgment, and breadth of vision—would be needed, and such representatives, he believed, would be forthcoming.[21]

To some degree the whole issue had been misunderstood, *The Federalist* argued. The destabilizing effect of clashing factions—a notorious flaw in popular governments—did not apply in such a large-scale republican nation as the United States. In fact the opposite was true. For the larger the society, Madison most famously wrote, "provided it lie within a practicable sphere" in which the bond between ruler and ruled could be maintained, the safer all would be. The multiplicity of factions would make it unlikely that any one group or combination of groups could overwhelm the others. In a large republican nation the grinding struggle of interests will tend to splinter factional coalitions; fragmentation would deflect what he called "plans of oppression." In effect passion and interest would create their own remedy. "Extend the sphere," Madison wrote in the most famous passage of the *Federalist* papers,

> and you take in a greater variety of parties and interests; you make it less probable that a majority of the whole will have a common motive to invade the rights of other citizens; or if such a common motive exists, it will be more difficult for all who feel it to discover their own strength, and to act in unison with each other.

But what would prevent one of the four elements of the federal government—the executive, the two branches of the legislature, and the judiciary—from dominating the others and thus establishing a one-sided, autocratic regime? It could not happen, *The Federalist* replied. Each branch of the federal government had powers that could negate those of the others, and all four overlapped in their powers sufficiently to brake the others' possible excesses.[22]

As for the absence of a Bill of Rights, Hamilton confronted the issue directly, in his own distinctive way. The Constitution itself, he argued, guaranteed essential rights—jury trials in criminal cases, habeas corpus, freedom from bills of attainder, from ex-post-facto laws, from religious tests for officeholding, and from titles of nobility. And quite aside from that, the concept was inapplicable. Bills of rights were "stipulations between kings and their subjects," in effect abridgments of royal prerogatives that had been fought for "sword in hand." Here the people have all the rights not explicitly surrendered in grants of power to the government. "Why declare that things shall not be done which there is no power to do?" To do so might well furnish ambitious men "a plausible pretence for claims to that power."[23]

And as for the most general concern of all, there was no reason, *The Federalist* wrote, why a centralized national government must be incompatible with personal liberty if, as the Constitution provided, that authority were limited to enumerated powers, all others being retained by the states and the people. If it ever happened that those restrictions, enforced by the courts, were ignored by federal officeholders, then the whole constitution of government would be at an end and private problems would scarcely matter in the general catastrophe that would result.

So in page after page (592 pages in all in the first book edition), in essay after essay, week after week through seven months while the fate of the nation hung in the balance, the authors of the *Federalist* papers, amid a bedlam of conflicting voices, explained and explored the Constitution, article by article, clause by clause—the need for it, its powers and limitations, and its proof against the attacks aimed to defeat it. But in explaining the document and the government it would create, the *Federalist* authors, impelled by the urgency they felt and the complexity of reconciling radical ideals of political liberty with the present need for power, went beyond the range of familiar problems to reach a level of thought deeper and more original than that of any of the other pamphleteers and essayists. Pragmatically, unsystematically, almost inadvertently, they drew fundamental principles into the popular debate. They were not attempting to write a formal treatise on the foundations of government or to create a new science of politics. Their aim was simply to convince people whose minds and experiences were shaped by the Revolutionary ideology that the principles they revered, especially the preservation of private rights, would still apply under the powers of the new federal government. But doing so presented unexpected challenges, paradoxes, and dilemmas that forced them to think freshly and devise new formulations which enriched, elaborated, and deepened the political tradition they had inherited and continued to revere.

New phrases, fresh terms crop up in their defense of the Constitution, reflecting new angles of vision in approaching the problems of power. So Hamilton, insisting with increasing urgency that the two levels of government, states and nation, could coexist within the same territory without conflict, focused that famous issue on the distinction, familiar in law but not in political thought, between repugnance and concurrence. Jurisdictions that confronted each other, he argued, might, like conflicting laws, find their powers repugnant to each other. If that happened, a struggle would inevitably result until the dominance of one was somehow established. In a contest of governments this would mean nothing less than civil war. But repugnance was not inevitable. Two authorities with similar powers could concur, if their roles were clearly established—could divide their responsibilities into separate spheres—could even reinforce each other and clarify each other's role. The Constitution's federalist division of absolute powers was a structure of concurrence, he argued, not repugnancy. To understand that distinction was to understand the heart of the Constitution and the public world it would create.[24]

If the concept of repugnancy was misleading, so too was the doctrine, so celebrated by Thomas Paine in *Common Sense*, that simplicity in government was a virtue, complexity an unmitigated evil. The opposite, *The Federalist* argued, was true. For the simpler the structure of government, the more likely it was to be dominated by particular interests or individuals at the expense of others. Complexity not simplicity was needed to provide the institutional conditions for adversarial challenges, without which ambition could run free.

But the issue was more general than that. Complexity and adversarial institutions were instances of something broader. Tension—networks of tensions—was the fundamental necessity for free states. The whole of the Constitution, *The Federalist* made clear, was a great web of tensions, a system poised in tense equilibrium like the physical systems Newtonian mechanics had revealed. Administration within and among departments of free governments, Madison wrote, will have both the "means and the personal motives to resist encroachments of the others . . . Ambition must be made to counteract ambition." The organized competition of "opposite and rival interests" that is built into the Constitution, he believed, reflects "the whole system of human affairs, private as well as public." Pressures exerted at one point would activate rebalancing responses elsewhere; and it was in this mechanism of tense equilibria that Madison placed his hopes of protecting minorities from the impact of majoritarian rule.[25]

If for Hamilton the main problem was to convince a reluctant people that creating a centralized power complete with an army, commercial regulation, and taxation was both necessary and safe, for Madison the principal and much subtler problem was how to protect minority groups and individuals from the domination of majorities in control of a powerful, freely elected government. On the face of it, the problem was unsolvable: both legislative majoritarianism and private rights were ultimate values in free societies, and surely they contradicted each other. How could they coexist? One or the other would have to prevail: a choice was inescapable. But Madison refused to choose between them, and struggled to resolve the dilemma.

He had learned how difficult and yet how urgent the problem was as he had observed the evil effects of legislative majorities within some of the states over the previous five years. Again and again minority property rights had been overwhelmed by populist majorities. And he had good reason to anticipate that the same injustice would happen to other minorities—religious groups, whose plight he had seen at close hand in the recent struggle in Virginia to enact Jefferson's Act for Establishing Religious Freedom, and political dissidents. He took some comfort from the section of Article I that prohibited the states from impairing the obligation of contract and from issuing their own bills of credit and tender laws. And there were implicit reinforcements in the clauses that guaranteed to the states protection against violence that would threaten their republican integrity and bound the judges in every state to enforce the Constitution, the laws of Congress, and the treaties entered into by the United States. He believed too that the complicated amendment process would help block the domination of one or another passionate and well-organized group, and he expected the Senate to constrain the powers of majorities in the House.

But these institutional arrangements, he feared, would not be enough to protect minorities within the states. He had pondered the issue deeply, and by the time the Philadelphia convention met he had reached a conclusion, which he explained to Jefferson in the massive letter that became the basis for *Federalist* No. 10.

He was convinced, he wrote Jefferson in what he called an "immoderate digression," that the only true protection for minority rights threatened by majorities in the state assemblies was a veto by the federal Congress on legislation passed in the states—a "constitutional negative" that he believed would tend to be impartial because of the moderating effect of diversity at the national level. In the Philadelphia convention, he explained, he had argued that a congressional veto over state legislation was necessary "to secure individuals against encroachments on their rights." But to his great regret that effort had been defeated, and with that defeat had gone his hope for enforcing justice at the state level. But, one might ask—and he asked himself this—would not the federal judiciary "supply the place of a [congressional] negative on [the states'] laws"? Possibly, he wrote; but "it is more convenient to prevent the passage of a law than to declare it void after it passed," and in any case, would injured individuals within the states be in a position to carry suits against states up to the Supreme Court? And if they did, and if they won, would it not take the use of force by the federal government to impose a judicial ruling against an offending state? And was that not precisely what the Constitution had sought to avoid?

So in Philadelphia he had failed in his efforts to secure private rights within the states by placing them under the direct guardian-ship of the federal government. But that bitter experience had greatly sharpened his understanding of the general problem of minority rights, and he applied that understanding at the national level in *Federalist* No. 10 with a brilliance that would enlighten consti-tutional thought ever after. In that resonant essay, so much more insightful than Hamilton's *Federalist* No. 9, which dealt with similar problems, he explained, as no one else had done, how the extended nation's complex web of tensions would prevent a "common interest or passion" from creating "a majority . . . in an unjust pursuit" that would deprive individuals of their rights. Others had approached that insight, had written of the moderating effect of diversity, but had not grasped its importance, uncovered its inner logic, or explained its implications as Madison did. And the heart of his understanding lay in his instinctive sense of the balancing equilib-rium created by the interaction of contending forces.[26]

Tension, balance, adversarial clashes leading to conciliating mod-eration lay at the core of the *Federalist* writers' thought—but they knew that a mechanically tense, self-balancing system did not acti-vate or maintain itself. Its success would depend in the end on the character of the people who managed it and who allowed themselves to be ruled by it—their reasonableness, their common sense, their capacity to rise above partisan passions to act for the common good and remain faithful to constitutional limits. The *Federalist* authors shared the common belief that most people everywhere, in their deepest nature, are selfish and corruptible and that the desire for domination is so overwhelming that no one should be trusted with unqualified authority, but they were confident that under the Consti-tution's checks and balances power would not be unconfined, and for such a self-limiting system there would be virtue enough in the

American people for success. "As there is a degree of depravity in mankind," Madison wrote, "which requires a certain degree of circumspection and distrust, so there are other qualities in human nature which justify a certain portion of esteem and confidence." But it was Hamilton, in one of the last of the *Federalist* papers, who made the point most succinctly: "The supposition of universal venality in human nature," he wrote, "is little less an error in political reasoning than the supposition of universal rectitude. The institution of delegated power implies that there is a portion of virtue and honor among mankind, which may be a reasonable foundation of confidence. And experience justifies the theory."[27]

Goodwill and a degree of impartiality would always be needed. If every compromise is taken as a defeat that must be overturned, and if no healing generosity is ever shown to defeated rivals, the best-contrived constitution in the world would not succeed. Properly understood and faithfully adhered to, the Constitution, the *Federalist* writers explained, despite its possible imperfections, was a sensitive instrument for balancing power and liberty. And it is the detail, clarity, and fullness of their explanation of the Constitution's structure and the principles that underlay it, and their perceptiveness and shrewdness in analyzing the general problems of power and its dangers in human society, that has made *The Federalist* an enduring document.

For all its distance from us in time and culture, for all the changes that have overtaken the world since 1788, the *Federalist* papers remain relevant, and acutely relevant, because they address masterfully our permanent concerns with political power—under our Constitution and in general. The *Federalist* writers knew that a structure of power must exist in any stable, civilized society, but they knew too that power uncontrolled will certainly be abused. They had vividly in mind the principles of political freedom that had been formulated in the decade of pounding ideological debate before 1776 and that had been discussed again in the writing of the state constitutions in the years that followed. Defending the establishment of sufficient national power to sustain a stable and effective society, they sought to preserve the maximum range of personal rights consistent with it. In this fundamental concern for the balance of power and liberty—which had been the central theme of America's earlier struggle with Britain—the *Federalist* writers, conservators of what were then radical political principles, are our contemporaries. Their constitutional idiom is ours; their political problems at the deepest level are ours; and we share their cautious optimism that personal freedom and national power—the preservation of private rights and the maintenance of public safety—can be compatible. But maintaining that balance is still a struggle, in times of danger or disillusion a bitter struggle; and so we continue to look back to what these extraordinarily thoughtful men wrote so hurriedly under such intense pressure two centuries ago. The *Federalist* papers—not a theoretical treatise on political philosophy but a practical commentary on the uses and misuses of power—still speak to us directly.

# A Note on *The Federalist* and the Supreme Court

The chronology of the Supreme Court's citations of *The Federalist* is a significant commentary on the persistent relevance of the papers and the variety of purposes to which they have been put. As the numbers indicate, the greater the distance in time from the writing of the papers, the more the justices have found it useful to draw on the authority of this two-century-old commentary. In the first thirty years after the adoption of the Constitution many of the justices had themselves been members of the ratifying debates (Chief Justice John Jay had of course been one of the *Federalist* authors), and the papers' role as polemical briefs was still a living memory. They were seen as political arguments, however powerful, and had no aura of sanctity. Madison himself cautioned a correspondent against using the papers indiscriminately as an authority because the writers, he said, in their desperation, had been more zealous in their arguments than he would have liked.[28] Chief Justice John Marshall, who had been active in the Virginia ratifying convention, referred to *The Federalist* in *McCulloch v. Maryland*, but only to reject the defense attorneys' use of the papers. "No tribute can be paid to their [the *Federalist* authors'] worth," he wrote, "which exceeds their merit; but in applying their opinions to the cases which may arise in the progress of our government, a right to judge of their correctness must be retained." *The Federalist*, he felt, should not be blindly followed as an authority, though when he thought the papers were applicable to his arguments, he did not hesitate to use them. Thus Hamilton's *Federalist* No. 31, Marshall argued, clearly proved false the accusation that the federal government could or would deprive the states of the power to tax and collect revenue. "Had the authors of those excel-

lent essays been asked, whether they contended for that construction
of the constitution which would place within the reach of the states
those measures which the government might adopt for the execution
of its powers, no man who has read their instructive pages will hesitate to admit that their answer must have been in the negative." In
the anonymous newspaper essays he later wrote to defend *McCulloch*
Marshall again argued that many of the opponents of the decision
were using the *Federalist* essays incorrectly to support their cause. His
own citations were presumably correct, and later he joined Justices
Joseph Story and William Johnson in citations that set a precedent
for the role of *The Federalist* in High Court opinions.[29]

During the remainder of the nineteenth century and through the
1920s the justices cited the papers only occasionally—they appear in
between three and nine cases each decade. In those years counselors
pleading before the Court referred to the papers almost as frequently
as the justices. The reliance of the justices on the papers differed
markedly: Story (1811–45) cited the papers five times, Stephen Field
(1863–87) five times, and Melville Fuller (1888–1910) six times. But
Justices John Marshall Harlan (1877–1911) and Joseph McKenna
(1898–1925), who had similarly long terms on the bench, cited the
papers only twice and once, respectively. Throughout the nineteenth
century the most frequently cited *Federalist* essays were No. 32
(Hamilton, on exclusive and concurrent powers of taxation: eleven
citations by 1894) and No. 42 (Madison, on powers delegated to the
federal government: seven citations).[30]

In contrast to the reserve that Madison desired, the need for careful evaluation that Marshall advocated, and the infrequency of the
citations in the nineteenth century, twentieth-century justices have
shown little restraint in using the papers to support their opinions,
and increasingly as an irrefutable authority. Between 1930 and 1959
the number of cases per decade in which the justices cited *The Federalist* doubled over those of the preceding ten decades, and the rate
doubled again in the 1960s, and doubled yet again in the 1980s. And
the importance of the papers in these opinions and the reverence
with which they were treated grew with the number of citations. At

certain points *The Federalist* appears to have been a deciding factor in the justices' decisions.

Why the increase in citations, why the papers' increasing importance and sanctity? Not simply because of an increase in the number of cases disposed of by opinion—that number declined significantly in those years. And not because of the presence of self-described "originalists" on the Court for whose views *The Federalist,* might have been uniquely supportive. The two most vehement "originalists" on the Court at the end of the twentieth century, Justices Clarence Thomas and Antonin Scalia, have not led in citing *The Federalist,* though at times Justice Scalia has relied heavily on certain papers. In the cases between 1995 and 1999, in fact, Justice John Paul Stevens cited the papers more frequently than any of his colleagues; Justices Scalia, Anthony Kennedy, and Stephen Breyer made about the same number of references. Justices David Souter, William Rehnquist, and Sandra Day O'Connor ranked in the middle, and Justices Thomas and Ruth Bader Ginsburg, representing quite opposite views, have both cited the papers only once. It is suggestive, and perhaps consistent, that Thomas leads the Court overall in citations of the *Anti*-federalist papers (four citations, 1995–97), which he used to demonstrate the legitimacy of the Founders' fears of the federal government's power and his belief that they had not intended the central government to have as much power as it has today. (How the Antifederalists' views explain the Constitution that was adopted over their objections has not been made clear.) Other "originalists" and justices both conservative and liberal have also made use of the Antifederalist writings, though to a lesser extent.[31]

The protean quality of the *Federalist* papers and their importance as final authority on the Founders' intent becomes dramatic in situations where justices differ on the interpretation of particular essays within the same case. A notable early example is the differing interpretation of *Federalist* No. 38 by Justices Roger Taney and Benjamin Curtis in the 1857 Dred Scott decision. Both justices began with Madison's defense of congressional authority to form new states, but they applied the passage differently, consistent with their conflicting views of slaveholders' rights to bring slaves into territories where slavery was outlawed. In *Printz v. U.S.* (1997), which involved the constitutionality of handgun licensing and background checks in the Brady Act, the justices devoted much time disputing each other's interpretation of certain *Federalist* papers, each claiming the support of the papers' authority. Justice Scalia made use of several papers (Nos. 36, 45, 27, as well as an essay from "Brutus") in his opinion for the majority. In his dissent Justice Souter placed even more importance on *The Federalist,* going so far as to say, "In deciding these cases, which I have found closer than I had anticipated, it is The Federalist that finally determines my position. I believe that the most straightforward reading of No. 27 is authority for the Government's position here, and that this reading is both supported by No. 44 and consistent with Nos. 36 and 45." To this Justice O'Connor replied:

> Justice Souter contends that his interpretation of Federalist No. 27 is "supported by No. 44," written by Madison, wherefore he claims that "Madison and Hamilton" together stand opposed to our view. In fact, The Federalist No. 44 quite clearly contradicts Justice Souter's reading . . . Even if we agreed with Justice Souter's reading of The Federalist No. 27, it would still seem to us most peculiar to give the view expressed in that one piece, not clearly confirmed by any other writer, the determinative weight he does. That would be crediting the most expansive view of federal authority ever expressed, and from the pen of the most expansive expositor of federal power . . . More specifically, it is widely recognized that "The Federalist reads with a split personality" on matters of federalism . . . To choose Hamilton's view, as Justice Souter would, is to turn a blind eye to the fact that it was Madison's—not Hamilton's—that prevailed, not only at the Constitutional Convention and in popular sentiment, but in the subsequent struggle to fix the meaning of the Constitution by early congressional practice. [Citations omitted]

Souter responded that he believed there was

> support in Madison's No. 44 for the straightforward reading of Hamilton's No. 27 and, so, no occasion to discount the authority of Hamilton's views as expressed in The Federalist as somehow

reflecting the weaker side of a split constitutional personality. This, indeed, should not surprise us, for one of the Court's own authorities rejects the "split personality" notion of Hamilton and Madison as being at odds in The Federalist, in favor of a view of all three Federalist writers as constituting a single personality notable for its integration.[32]

Over the years, as respect for the papers' authority has grown, shifts in the selection of and emphases on particular papers that serve the justices' purposes have become notable, but so too has the absence of references to papers and arguments that the *Federalist* authors themselves believed to be fundamental. Their carefully wrought discussions of basic issues—democracy versus republicanism, the foundation principle of the separation of powers, the nature of political virtue, geographical extent and republican stability—have rarely been considered by the justices, while the technical passages on jurisdictional boundaries have been heavily emphasized. The first citation of Madison's most famous theoretical contribution, No. 10, on which a library of commentary has been written by twentieth-century students of political theory, appeared only in 1974—185 years after the Court first met. And the use made of it in fourteen cases between then and 2000 is a blur of offhand references, some irrelevant to the issue at hand, some inconsistent with previous citations of the same paper, almost all in support of arguments in favor of a free, unencumbered, unpreferential marketplace for rival interest groups, whether corporations or racial minorities.

Overall, for the Supreme Court justices *The Federalist* has never been a treatise on political theory or a masterwork on political science, but a guide to the disposition of power in specific circumstances, an authority on the constitutional use of force and the constraints on the use of force in the intricate functioning of the federalist system of government in America. As these questions grew in complexity and importance in the late twentieth century, so too did the need for an authentic voice of the founding generation to guide the reasoning of the nation's final arbiters of the legitimate use of power.

# V

# Atlantic Dimensions

It is difficult to convey the energy and imagination that went into the constitutional creations of the Revolutionary generation—the freshness of the Revolutionary leaders' minds, their capacity to re-imagine the political world. Yet these were not intellectuals devoted to ideas as such; they were not scholars engaged in the systematic study of political and constitutional thought, or philosophers debating the details of formal discourses. They were intelligent, well-educated provincials—merchants, planters, lawyers, and politicians—coping with the manifest problems of public authority that faced them, referring back for guidance to their own experience and the traditions they knew, rejecting some ideas and institutions and modifying others to suit their needs, and propelled into new ways of thinking and new forms of public organization not by the desire for innovation but by logical necessity, by the attraction of the possibilities they could see, and by the sheer momentum of their efforts. The result, in these provincial states and in the American nation, was a new configuration of public authority and a new set of constitutional procedures which in a short period of years resonated throughout the Atlantic world.

It is now conventional among historians who consider what has been called the age of the democratic revolutions to say that after a

brief flurry in the first two years of the French Revolution the constitutional ideas and institutions of the American Revolution had
little influence on the development of European or Latin American
constitutionalism—that the struggles there were on issues largely
defined by the ideas and experience of the French Revolution, and
that in any case conditions of public life elsewhere in the Atlantic
world were so different from those in the United States that
any attempt to transplant American institutions was doomed to
failure.

And there is no doubt that the basic conditions of public life in
North America were unique. There, there had been neither a deeply
instituted monarchy, nor legally constituted social orders, nor an
effectively established state church to contend with. Nor had there
been a deeply entrenched bureaucratic state apparatus, as distinct
from government. The national government, in the Revolutionary
decade, had been built from the bottom up, with local bodies parsi-
moniously endowing higher echelons with exiguous powers, so that
not only was the structure as a whole fragile but its ultimate authority was no more than a bundle of concessions subject to withdrawal.
The main evidence that there was a national government was, for
the merchants and port officials, the presence of customs collectors
(who were usually dependents of the merchants) and, for all others,
the workings of the post office.

Yet, despite this, the interest in American constitutionalism was
intense throughout the Atlantic world in the revolutionary years; and
in the generations that followed it remained deeply embedded in the
awareness of political leaders, publicists, and intellectuals. How
much so appears at times in strange and startling ways.

In the early editions of the Abbé Raynal's wildly popular *Histoire
philosophique et politique . . . des Européens dans les deux Indes,* provincial
North America, its people, institutions, and lifeways, had been
demeaned in the manner of Buffon, but in his revision of 1780, Raynal celebrated the new nation in rhapsodies. He now confessed that
he palpitated with joy, "eyes floating in delicious tears," in contemplating that "heroic country" and its public laws, that "retreat of tol-

eration, of manners, of laws, of virtue, and of freedom."[1] Talleyrand, who so greatly admired the *Federalist* papers, was no one to dis-
solve into tearful ecstasies, but even he was moved to superlatives in
contemplating the American scene. The three greatest men of his
epoch, he was quoted as saying, were Napoleon, Pitt, and Alexander
Hamilton, and of the three he gave first place to Hamilton. One
wonders how the son of the Norwegian constitutionalist Falsen (who
copied parts of the Massachusetts constitution directly into the Norwegian constitution) fared with his given names: George Benjamin—
or what the Grand Duke Leopold of Tuscany, bombarded by advice
on state affairs by his father, the Emperor Francis, and his mother,
Maria Theresa, made of the copy of the Virginia constitution presented to him by Filippo Mazzei.[2]

Brazilian intellectuals, discontented and contemplating reform,
secretly sought out Jefferson in France for confidential advice, and, as
overseas students at the University of Coimbra, devoured accounts of
the American Revolution and of its constitutional innovations. Their
strange colleague, the martyr of Brazil's aborted rebellion of 1789 in
the inland province of Minas Gerais, Joaquim José da Silva Xavier,
kept in his pocket a copy of the French translations of the American
state constitutions, though knowing no French he had to ask others to
translate it for him. The Prussian Kantian Friedrich von Gentz was so
impressed by what he discovered of American constitutionalism that
he dedicated himself to exploring it at length in a comparative study
of the American and French Revolutions—a treatise that John
Quincy Adams enthusiastically translated into English for American
consumption. The Venezuelans, in 1811, under the influence of Fran-
cisco Miranda, an enthusiast of the American Revolution, made
plans to issue their own declaration of independence on the precise
anniversary of Jefferson's, but missed by twenty-four hours.[3]

That Raynal and Talleyrand in France, Falsen in Norway, Gentz in
Prussia, Silva Xavier in Brazil, and Miranda in Venezuela were well
aware of American constitutionalism and sought to explore it and

to some extent promote it is less mysterious when viewed in the light
of the extraordinary speed with which notice of America's innovations coursed through the Atlantic communities, metropolitan and
colonial.

It is not surprising that the Declaration of Independence was circulating in England within a month of its publication; but it is surprising that it appeared simultaneously in French in a Dutch journal,
and then repeatedly in a series of French periodicals—in all, there
would be at least nine different French translations before 1783. By
October 1776 the Declaration was available in Basel in a German
translation of a French translation, which was followed the next year
by another, partial German translation, based on another French
version, by one Matthias Sprengel. And that is a curious document.
Sprengel, being a cautious Hanoverian fearful of spreading sedition
and offending his king, first omitted the Declaration's preamble as
not being important, and then substituted "regime" (*Regierung*) for
the "He" of Jefferson's enumerated charges against the king, thus
vaguely identifying the accused as someone or something feminine
("She imposed taxes on us against our will [Sie hat uns Taxen wider
unsere Einwilligung aufgelegt]").[4]

By then, in early 1777, Franklin had arrived in France, and the
major phase of the circulation of American public documents
began. Working with great speed, he published a French translation
of the copy of the Articles of Confederation that he carried with him
(it was a preliminary, incomplete, confidential draft, different from
the document that would be adopted by Congress in 1781), and it is
in the form of a retranslation back into English of that French translation that the Articles of Confederation first appeared in England.
And then, in a bizarre twist, that English version of a French translation of a misleading American original became the source of several
*new* French translations that quickly appeared in various French
periodicals.[5]

By mid-1777, only a year after American independence had been
declared, the state constitutions and bills of rights had begun to
appear in Europe—some in English in John Almon's *Remembrancer,*

others in French in La Rochefoucauld and Franklin's *Affaires de l'Angleterre et de l'Amérique*. That collection—curiously inaccurate since much of it was copied from the *Remembrancer* which had left blanks in place of derogatory references to the crown and Parliament—proved to be a preliminary version of La Rochefoucauld's major publication, the *Recueil* of 1778. That popular miscellany of Americana included, besides various enactments of the Continental Congress and, strangely, Harvard's honorary degree encomium to Washington, the texts of the constitutions of all the new American states—documents, La Rochefoucauld declared, that were "the finest monuments of human wisdom. They constitute the purest democracy which has ever existed; they already appear to be achieving the happiness of the people who have adopted them, and they will forever constitute the glory of the virtuous men who conceived them."[6]

By then a variety of European presses were turning out French and German versions of the state constitutions and the Articles of Confederation in a maze of translations, retranslations, summaries, and digests, all of which were read, Franklin reported, "with rapture," and which nourished intense discussions among the French intelligentsia and liberal politicians, on the constitutional principles of ideal states and the possibilities of reform. German translators relied on French translations that appeared not only in French periodicals but in Leiden's *Gazette*. Van der Kemp in Holland, inspired by John Adams, produced in Dutch what he called a collection of pieces drawn from a variety of American and French sources. By 1783 La Rochefoucauld had produced a French translation of the official Articles of Confederation that had finally been adopted by Congress. In 1785 Franklin sponsored a bulky, comprehensive German translation of the French versions of all the American state constitutions. And then, in 1787, translations of the federal Constitution in both German and French began their circulation through Europe—in Hamburg within a month of the Constitution's initial publication in Philadelphia, in Brussels and Leiden within two months, and in Paris early in 1788. In 1792 the *Federalist* papers were published, and quickly republished, in a full French translation that was so well received that its two main authors were given honorary French citizenship by a nation "made free by their guiding light and courage." Later in the 1790s, Spanish versions of the American documents began to appear. By 1798 copies of the American Constitution were being published in Spanish in the West Indies, and by 1811 all the constitutional documents, from the Declaration of Independence to the state constitutions together with extracts from Paine's writings, Washington's Farewell Address, and Jefferson's first inaugural address were available in Spanish, and newspapers in Caracas, Buenos Aires, Mexico City, and Santiago were carrying excerpts and commentaries.[7]

Thus awareness of provincial America, its successful revolution and constitutional creations, had quickly become part of the consciousness of officialdom and the clerisy in both cosmopolitan Europe and its colonial dependencies. But with what consequence? The *general* effect of the American Revolution throughout the Atlantic world is well known: its creation of the sense that a new era was beginning, its amplification and embodiment of the ideas of liberty and equality, its legitimation of criticism of existing powers.[8] But what *specific* difference did the American constitutional reforms, the American constitutional presence, make? How can one assess the specific role that American constitutionalism played in the seismic transformation of power relations that took place throughout the Atlantic world in the age of revolution?

An indication appears in the famous chain of polemics that began with the publication in 1776 of Richard Price's pamphlet *Observations on the Nature of Civil Liberty . . . and the Justice and Policy of the War with America* and that continued in a series of linked publications by Franklin, Turgot, John Adams, the Abbé Mably, Condorcet, Mazzei, and the American pamphleteer John Stevens, before subsiding, after twelve years, just before the outbreak of the French Revolution.

What is most striking, and suggestive, in this series of exchanges is the progressive narrowing of the issues at stake and the ultimate focus of concern. Price's *Observations,* which went through twenty-three printings in the English-speaking world, France, and the Netherlands, was not only a systematic defense of the American cause but a wide-swinging, broadside challenge to Britain's political establishment. Price's first target was the House of Commons, whose corruptions he would totally purge. That led to proposals to reform the entire system of parliamentary representation, to establish the sovereignty of the people, to a denial of any nation's right to assert authority over any other, and to the idea of a Congress of Europe whose decisions would be enforced by a European army. For this comprehensive challenge to the status quo Price was attacked by a host of writers, some as respectable as the Archbishop of York, some as disreputable as the hired hack Dr. Shebbeare. Franklin, like every dissident, rejoiced, and passed on a copy of the pamphlet to Turgot, Louis XVI's chief minister, physiocrat, and financial reformer.

Turgot's reply to Price, written two years later but published only in 1784, began the process of narrowing the debate to a single issue. For while he too ranged across the whole field of reform, the nature of liberty, and sound public policy, he took the occasion to expose what he believed were the basic flaws in the American state constitutions. They were, he wrote, simply slavish imitations of England's constitution in their bicameralism and separation of powers; and the nation itself was, like the Netherlands, no more than an "aggregate of parts," every state having taxing powers over the goods of all others and its own system of commercial regulation. Such a nation, resting on "the false basis of very ancient and very vulgar policy," was no consolidated body "*one* and homogeneous," as a nation should be. The future would be grim, he warned, if these errors, and especially the checks and balances in the state constitutions, were not corrected.[9]

By the time Turgot's letter was published, the issue of distributive versus unified constitutional powers had become a core issue. The elderly philosopher Mably, in four public letters addressed to his friend John Adams, declared himself in favor of Adams's constitution of Massachusetts because, he believed, its bicameralism constrained the force of democracy (ignoring the fact that the document also provided for the popular election of all state officials and a wide electoral franchise). For this, in France, he was denounced as an ideological aristocrat, though in fact he feared aristocracies of either birth or wealth and sought ways to limit their force.

By then, with the central issue increasingly focused on aristocracies and the dangers they posed, John Adams was at work on his massive defense of the bicameralism of the now famous, to some notorious, constitution he had written for his native state. In his prodigious, three-volume *Defence of the Constitutions of . . . the United States*—that formidable encyclopedia of constitutionalism past and present—Adams threw the weight of the whole record of constitutionalism in Western civilization into the defense of bicameralism. For him this was no technical problem of constitutional architecture; it involved nothing less than the nature of political man and the inescapable propensity of all societies to develop differential and invidious levels of wealth, intellect, and power. Equality could not be mandated. The problem was how to keep the upper echelons— aristocrats, plutocrats, nobles—from overwhelming and contaminating the entire body politic. That could be achieved, he wrote, only by sealing them off in their own organ of government, with powers defined and limited. Bicameralism, far from being a denial of popular liberties by perpetuating aristocracies, was the ultimate protector of freedom by confining society's most ambitious and dangerous forces to bounded fields of action.[10]

Within a year, the responses began to appear. The critical document proved to be John Stevens's *Observations on Government*, a belligerent attack on what he called the "rubbage" of Adams's *Defence*, its "absurdities and inconsistencies" dredged up "from the storehouses and magazines of antiquity," its bicameralism a "single remedy for all disorders" concocted out of the delusion that America had, or ever could have, any "orders, ranks, or nobility." Madison had sent a copy of Stevens's blistering polemic, which had its own version of the separation of powers, to Mazzei, from whom it passed to Condorcet and Du Pont. All three immediately saw the pamphlet's potential for supporting their attack on bicameralism, hence institutionalized aristocracy, despite the fact that Stevens objected not to Adams's bicameralism as such but to his assumption that aristocracies were inevitable, that future societies, like those in the past, would always generate dangerous, privileged elites whose destructive influence would have to be isolated and confined. For Condorcet and Mazzei, who had no way of separating out the functional from the social role of legislative organs, this was precisely the point. They immediately translated Stevens's 56-page pamphlet into French, adding 224 pages of their own, in which they explained at length the importance of this American challenge to Adams for what they saw as the main problem of enlightened reform in France.[11]

The two had already entered the battle in Mazzei's four-volume *Recherches historiques* of 1788, which included, besides an entire section devoted to an attack on Mably as a crypto-aristocrat, the text of Condorcet's "Quatre Lettres d'un bourgeois de New-Haven." Mably, Mazzei wrote, not only shamelessly favored the constitutional rights of the rich over those of ordinary people, but in his praise of Massachusetts's bicameral constitution for peacefully preparing the way for the inevitable emergence of an aristocratic state (as opposed to Pennsylvania's unicameralism, which Mably believed would surely lead to convulsions, oligarchy, and tyranny)—in all of this, Mazzei wrote, Mably was technically misinformed and conceptually deluded. Condorcet concurred, and demonstrated at length in the fourth of his "Lettres" the dangers of a divided legislature and the ways in which a single assembly representing the whole nation could be stabilized and perpetuated by frequent elections, referendums, declarations of human rights, and voter initiatives. Though he would limit the franchise to property holders, Condorcet advocated the abolition of all hereditary distinctions, making all offices elective, and prohibiting government regulations of all kinds. Americans, he concluded, are not sophisticated people, but their "naive expression" of the few maxims on which they based their peace and happiness express the common sense of all mankind, which is in its nature opposed to "those complex machines . . . where so many counterweights are supposed to produce a balance."[12]

In the course of this decade-long flurry of publications, Price's

scattered attack on the whole establishment of his time had come to
rest on the single issue of aristocracy and its role in the constitutional
structure of enlightened states. In America, given the structure of
colonial society, aristocracy had been a peripheral—though to some,
like Jefferson, a significant—issue, but it was a fundamental social
problem in European life and became a structural problem in European constitutionalism. Involving as it did the inescapable, glaring
issue of privilege and social oppression, it lay at the heart of the
struggles in public life and dominated the debates on the forms of
public institutions.

In all of this, for Turgot and Condorcet as for Mably, the American
experience was peculiarly instructive.

Instructive—and exemplary. Provincial America, removed from
the layered complexities of European life and the intricate racial
structuring of Latin American society and having experimented with
modes of enlightened constitutionalism, provided living examples: of
what might be done, of the dangers that might be avoided, of alter-
natives that might be explored. American constitutionalism was not
a theory to be debated or a model to be imitated but a reserve of
experience—exemplary, of good or ill—a reserve that could be
drawn on when needed, intermittently, selectively, with emphases
that were shaped differently by the distinctive problems of different
societies in different modes and at different stages of transformation
in the age of the Atlantic revolutions.

Thus for the English radicals of the 1790s—Cartwright, Cobbett,
Hardy, Paine, Cooper, Hartley, Horne Tooke, Yorke, Spence—
American constitutionalism, however "limited, cerebral, and middle
class" it may have been, was drawn upon, was the inspiration for, and
became the natural bridge to the populist, plebeian radicalism that
lay behind the making of the English working class. Exaggerating
the radicalism of American constitutional ideals and principles, they
adopted into their own program the idea of written constitutions
antecedent to all government and empowered by constituent assem-

blies; the notion that the people and not institutions were sovereign; that government in all its parts should be representative of the people; and that adult male suffrage should be universal.

But beyond that, and more important, for them America's reform of public institutions was dynamic; its inner propulsion led not simply to liberalizing the institutions of public authority but to confronting social concerns and alleviating social oppression. Just as all the leading radicals agreed with John Cartwright that America had become England's best instructor "in the . . . recovering from that state of corruption of which the constitution is sick at heart," so they agreed with Paine that social benefits flowed directly from political liberty. America, Paine wrote, proved that republicanism and popular sovereignty promoted the general welfare; in such regimes the poor are not oppressed and the rich are not privileged. So too Thomas Cooper saw in America proof that republicanism in its nature promoted agrarian justice. And again and again the London Corresponding Society "pointed to America to show that constitutional reform would ease the people's suffering as well as guarantee their liberties."[13]

These passionate English reformers—frustrated and harassed by the establishment, some tried for treason—found within America's constitutionalism a deeper purpose that inspired the march toward radical social goals.

The French, in the same critical years of the 1790s, needed no external stimulus to social reform. But *their* policy struggles centered on precisely the issues of American constitutionalism that the *philosophes* and liberal politicians had been debating since 1776. On the two major issues in the critical debates during the first months of the National Assembly, American examples were drawn upon, selectively—praised by some, denounced by others.

That France would adopt a Declaration of the Rights of Man and of Citizen was never in question, but its relation to the American state bills of rights which inspired it, and to Virginia's Declaration of Rights in particular, is significant. The structure of Virginia's Declaration (whose author, Condorcet wrote, deserves "the eternal gratitude of mankind") and that of the French Assembly, and the sequence of provisions in the two documents, are remarkably similar. But out of the necessity to repudiate deeply entrenched and legalized privileges, the French Declaration is more specific and insistent in defining human rights, the supremacy of law, and the nature of citizenship. Out of respect for the currents of religious skepticism and anticlericalism, it is more deistic and less doctrinally Christian. And out of deference to the tradition of French criminal law, it is more general in its provisions for procedural due process.

Once the Declaration was accepted the Assembly turned to the basic structure of a national constitution, and throughout the ensuing struggle the American experience was never far from the surface of the antagonists' minds. The initial proposal, by Jean-Joseph Mounier, for the separation and balance of powers among king, a Senate of royally appointed lifetime members, and representatives, was recognized by all as Anglo-American, if not purely English, in its essence. Perhaps, Mounier explained, America in 1776 had been a constitutional tabula rasa, but France in 1789 certainly was not; and though he, like his main opponent, the Abbé Sieyès, would eliminate aristocratic privileges, the monarchy, he insisted, still existed and somehow had to be accounted for. Again and again in arguing the case for bicameralism and the distribution and balance of powers, he and such supporters as Mirabeau, La Rochefoucauld, and Rabaut Saint-Etienne cited America's national and state constitutions, drew on the authority of Jefferson, and echoed the views of Adams.

Sieyès, in arguing successfully for a unicameral legislature and a limited, suspensive veto, reviewed the differences, point by point, between the existential, pre-existing republicanism of the American people and monarchical, aristocratic France. He and the other unicameralists, besides arguing the logic of their case and its congruence with the actualities of French society, noted the absence of a veto in Virginia's constitution, drew on Stevens's rebuttal of Adams, which they assumed was an attack on bicameralism, and the comments of Stevens's French collaborators, and argued again and again that France was not America where an upper house and executive veto did not threaten to perpetuate monarchy and aristocratic rule. Massachusetts and the American nation may have a strong executive, Sieyès insisted, but a governor or president, unlike the king, could be voted out of office, and there was no danger that an upper house might be dominated by a *noblesse* struggling to survive or some other special "order" or "estate."[14]

By 1794, as the French Revolution proceeded through its subsequent turmoils, the relevance of American constitutionalism faded in importance. But it had been crucial in the early, defining months—as, in distinctive ways, it was elsewhere throughout the Atlantic world.

For if the social implications of American constitutionalism were critical for the English radicals, and if defining human rights and assessing the benefits and dangers of balancing powers were critical for the French revolutionaries, American federalism proved to be a primary concern for nations as different as Switzerland and Argentina, attempting to reconstruct their public institutions—in the one case after Napoleon's imposition of the Helvetic Republic, in the other after the overthrow of Iberian imperialism.

For Switzerland, the dominant public issue for fifty years after Napoleon's conquest of 1798 was the struggle between, on the one hand, conservatives seeking to maintain the traditional autonomy of the cantons together with the patriarchal social order within them, and, on the other, progressives seeking broader powers for the central government and more equal social and political rights. And in all the immensely complex drafting and redrafting of constitutions and the rocketing back and forth between the two sides, American constitutions and American authorities and formulations were cited, quoted, and imitated—at times in astonishing detail, and also with much confusion. For such were the apparent ambiguities of the American system that both sides could, and did, claim its authority: the cantonists for the survival of states' rights in the American federalist system, the centralists for the supremacy of Congress, the president, and the federal courts. When one side claimed an advantage by association with the United States, the other, which in different circumstances was equally pro-American, ridiculed any supposed analogies.

Thus the ultracentralist Jean-Jacques Cart, once a resident of

Boston and New York and a devoted Americanist, fearing the force of his conservative opponents' efforts to emulate American federalism, declared that to "dress [Switzerland] up as the United States . . . would be to wrap up a pygmy in the garb of a giant. The trousers would be longer than the legs. He could not walk." To federalize "poor little Switzerland," he wrote, "would be absurd . . . strike out the term canton from the Helvetic dictionary. Strike it out for ever."

But it was not struck out. Though the Act of Mediation of 1803 created a more centralized state, the cantonal powers were restored in the Federal Pact of 1815, together with restrictions on political rights. That pact was immediately attacked by the philo-American Helvetic Society whose leaders called it a "political bastard" and declared (remarkably—this was 1830) that all Swiss governments must be "of the people, by the people, and for the people" ("aus dem Volke, durch das Volk, und für das Volk"). The restoration of more liberal institutions in 1830 led to even more elaborate examinations of American federalism in an outpouring of pamphlets, articles, and speeches. One side's declaration that "a government similar to that of the United States would suit our ancient confederation just as well as it suits those young and wise republics" was denounced by the other as "insidious," "dictatorial," and destructive to cantonal sovereignty—not because they objected to the American model in general (in fact they admired its decentralization) but because they feared presidential power in particular.

Through all this dense maze of polemics and proposals, much of it tangles of interpretations of American constitutionalism, there were powerful forces for compromise, which was achieved at last in the complex bicameral federalist system of Switzerland's long-lasting *Eidgenossenschaft*. That outcome was largely the work of the libertarian philosopher Troxler, who wrote,

> The constitution of the United States of America is a great work of art which the human mind created according to the eternal laws of its divine nature . . . It is a model and a pattern for the organization of the public life of republics in general, in which the whole and the parts shall both be free and equal . . . The

problem has been solved by the new world for all peoples, states and countries.[15]

There were similar encomia, though in far more bitterly contested circumstances, four thousand miles to the west. In the emerging nations of Latin America—sprawling, undeveloped, multiracial, politically chaotic at times to the point of anarchy—federalism was not a theoretical issue of choice. It was an inescapable structural problem in all of Spain's former provinces and territories as they groped, amid the blood-stained rubble of imperial rule and the ferocious ambitions of the caudillos, for ways to form stable, peaceful regimes. There were no autochthonous, pre-existing quasi-national units to declare their independence of alien powers and to evolve naturally into viable nation states. There were only larger or smaller jurisdictions whose legitimacy vanished with Spanish rule. As a result the basic struggle everywhere, once the Spanish troops were defeated, was to bring together whatever elements of authority there were—mainly cities and provinces—into combinations that would agree to share in a common authority. Federalism was therefore a fact before it was a theory.[16]

As the chaotic process of state formation in Latin America proceeded, realpolitik was everywhere, often in the crudest, most brutal form; but so too were idealistic hopes for enlightened, liberal polities. And those enlightened aspirations were rationalized and conceptualized with reference, in part to the classic texts of advanced European thought, in part to Hispanic traditions, and in large part to the widely circulating translations of North American constitutions, state and federal, with their emphasis on federalism.

The impact of North American constitutionalism on Latin America was profound, but often it was, as one historian, paraphrasing Isabel Allende, put it: like a lock ordered by catalogue that arrived with wrong instructions and no keys. That was certainly the view of Simón Bolívar, convinced that the federalism of the first Venezuelan constitution of 1811, modeled in part on the American Constitution, was a tragic mistake, responsible for the rebel government's failure and the slaughter of the counterrevolution that followed. What was needed for his countrymen, he believed—deeply divided as they were by race, class, and fiercely defended private jurisdictions; ignorant people for the most part, widely scattered and now caught up in a war to the death—was not multiple sovereignties (that idea, he wrote, was one of those "picturesque ideologies" produced by a "craze for imitation") but an all-powerful central government controlled by a decisive executive backed by force and capable of compelling scattered elements to coalesce. Like San Martín, who said he might die whenever he heard a countryman praising federalism, Bolívar believed that "only concentration has infused respect." Most often, in the end, in Venezuela and elsewhere, after years of chaos and successions of unstable regimes, that view prevailed in the predominance of innumerable dictators serving their own purposes on the way to public order.[17]

Yet to protect the endemic federalism, deeply rooted in the pre-independence diversity of the new nations, remained the goal of many enlightened reformers. At certain times and certain places that goal was reached by regional leaders determined to break the political and economic monopolies that had been established by force.

In Chile in the 1820s provincial leaders, reacting against the centralism of the earliest independent regimes, supported a federalist constitution for which that of the United States was an "archetype and example," and achieved a measure of distributed power, until conservatives, after a bitter civil war, imposed a tightly focused centralist regime. Ecuador's leading public intellectual, Vicente Rocafuerte, who in exile in Philadelphia had translated the major American state papers as well as *Common Sense* and who had described the Declaration of Independence as a political decalogue and the United States Constitution as "the only hope of an oppressed people," explained the ways in which his country's initial constitution was a deliberate imitation of the United States's, though every element in it, and especially its federalism, was debated, ridiculed, and praised. Uruguay's leaders designed what they called a "firm league of friendship" among its constituent parts that was modeled explicitly on the Articles of Confederation, and while their effort failed, elements of the Articles, discarded in the United States as a design for too loose a union, survived. And in Mexico, where the United States was initially an exciting symbol of liberty and prosperity, the fiscal and military quasi-independence of the provincial states was retained in the pact of 1823 and the federalist constitution of 1824, which combined elements of the United States Constitution and of Spain's liberal Cádiz constitution of 1812.[18]

But it was in Argentina, after years of civil war between *federales* and *unitarios* during which innumerable constitutions failed to establish authority superior to the provinces, that federalism, modeled on that of the United States even to the point of verbal quotation, was most clearly established. The leading theorist of Argentine federalism, Juan Bautista Alberdi, who has been described as a Hamiltonian, likened the United States in 1782 to Argentina in 1852: both anticipated the creation of national states that balanced central and regional powers. The resulting constitution of 1853 and the subsequent rule of Sarmiento vindicated the belief of would-be reformers throughout Latin America that federalism, when sufficiently modified to accommodate local needs, could become the mechanism for national integration and the basis for social and economic development.[19]

Argentina's integrative federalism would have its share of disruptions thereafter, but its success, in the lurching, chaotic development of the emerging nations of Latin America, was exemplary. Throughout the continent the hopes for some such resolution, based in part on the constitutional experience of North America, had been ubiquitous from the start. The northern model was experimented with, often disastrously, in country after country, emulated and rejected, but from the beginning it had *been* there—an essential, if endlessly disputed, resource, a central force in the continent's public life.

By mid-century the influence of American constitutionalism had reached not only the far southern boundaries of the Atlantic world but also its eastern extremities, in the German principalities, where it had once seemed largely irrelevant.

Though in the 1790s numerous German newspapers, pamphlets, and books had carried notices of the Anglo-American conflict, often distorted, and translations of certain key documents had been available, it was not until 1800, with the publication of Friedrich von Gentz's comparative study of the American and French revolutions—the study that had caught the eye of Quincy Adams—that the importance of American constitutionalism was presented in systematic form, and not until 1824, with the publication of Robert von Mohl's examination of America's "*Bundes-Staatsrecht*," that the entire machinery of American constitutionalism (the "miracle of our times," Mohl called it) was fully explored and its relevance to the German states clearly seen. Thereafter, with the rapid growth of interest in the possibility of a German confederation, more and more attention was devoted to the American model. Encyclopedias carried freshly written accounts, the translation of Tocqueville's *Democracy in America* went through thirteen printings before 1850, and the *Federalist* papers circulated widely, as did copies of the American Constitution. By 1848, when the German Constituent Assembly met in Frankfurt to frame a confederate state, a professor in that city could write: "The American name . . . never stood higher, everywhere are works and pamphlets in bookstores and on center tables in our institutions, and almost every orator points to them as a glorious example."[20]

And indeed much of the discussion in the Frankfurt Assembly focused on American constitutionalism—its federalism, its protection of rights, its system of representation, its separation of church and state, and its management of the military and foreign affairs. Though in the end the differences between the United States, protected by the Atlantic moat, and Germany as a collection not of republics but of monarchies, came to dominate the debate—and though in any case the Frankfurt Constitution was ultimately rejected—that assembly, even more than the French Constitutional Assembly of 1848, where American constitutionalism was also extensively discussed, marked the ultimate influence of American constitutionalism within the living memory of the Revolutionary generation.[21]

.   .   .

In the generations that have followed, that influence has remained pervasive—not merely in the design of specific constitutions but mainly and increasingly, as America's power has grown, in its embodiment of established Western values.

Two centuries after its creation by provincials developing the minority ideas of the Commonwealthmen, American constitutionalism, having radiated throughout the Atlantic world, has become a classic formulation for the world at large of effectiveness and constraint in the humane uses of power. But like all classic formulations, it has been and is now being questioned by people with other values, other aspirations, other beliefs in the proper uses of power—people who do not believe with Tocqueville and Troxler that American constitutionalism is a "work of art" or with Condorcet that the rights embedded in the American Constitution are "the natural rights of humanity," and who emphatically challenge Jefferson's belief that it is America's destiny to extend to other regions of the earth what he called "the sacred fire of freedom and self-government."[22]

Those challenges will continue and will intensify in the years ahead, but I think an equally important challenge is our own responsibility to probe the character of our constitutional establishment, as the eighteenth-century provincials probed the establishment they faced, to recognize that for many in our own time and within our own culture, it has become scholastic in its elaboration, self-absorbed, self-centered, and in significant ways distant from the ordinary facts of life.

And so one thinks back with increasing respect to the words of that worthy Connecticut jurist Oliver Ellsworth, who insisted that it is not enough to *say* that the traditional principles of political thought are irrefutable. One needs to know *why*. One needs "some reason."

# Notes

CHAPTER I

1. "History and the Creative Imagination" (Lewin Lecture, Washington University, St. Louis, 1985).

2. Julian P. Boyd, et al., eds., *The Papers of Thomas Jefferson* (Princeton, N.J., 1950–), II, 546 (punctuation slightly altered).

3. Clark, "Provincialism" was first published as the Presidential Address to the English Association, November 1962, and then reprinted in his essay collection *Moments of Vision* (London, 1981), pp. 50–62. It thereafter inspired an elaborate commentary by Enrico Castelnuovo and Carlo Ginzburg that appeared in Italian, French, and English: "Centro e periferia," in *Storia dell'arte italiana*, I (*Questione e metodi*) (Turin, 1979), 285–354; "Domination symbolique et geographie artistique dans l'art Italien," in *Actes de la recherche en sciences sociales*, 40 (1981), 51–72; and "Centre and Periphery," trans. Ellen Bianchini, in *History of Italian Art* (Cambridge, England, 1994), I, 29–112 (thanks to David J. Steinberg).

4. Kenneth A. Lockridge, *The Diary and Life of William Byrd II of Virginia, 1674–1744* (Chapel Hill, N.C., 1987), pp. 2–6, 46, 49–50, 123.

5. Frederick B. Tolles, *James Logan and the Culture of Provincial America* (Boston, 1957), pp. 191–94, chap. xii; David S. Shields, *Civil Tongues & Polite Letters in British America* (Chapel Hill, N.C., 1997), pp. xiv, xxv, 12, 32, 277 ff., 286, 297, 298.

6. Franklin to Mary Stevenson, Philadelphia, March 25, 1763, Leonard W. Labaree et al., eds., *The Papers of Benjamin Franklin* (New Haven, Conn., 1959–), X, 232–33. Cf. Kenneth Silverman, *A Cultural History of the American Revolution* (New York, 1976), p. 68: America's "nursling of English culture . . . drew its tastes and ideas from the mother country and from

Europe [and] gave back little if anything. . . . America in 1763 had still to acquire for the first time most of the features of metropolitan cultural life. . . . no one aimed very high or created with much urgency. At its core, American culture lacked ambition and focus, the sense of a subject."

7. Bailyn, *Faces of Revolution: Personalities and Themes in the Struggle for American Independence* (New York, 1990), p. 8.

8. David Cecil, *Melbourne* ([London, 1939, 1954] Indianapolis, 1954), p. 15.

9. Alan Everitt, *Change in the Provinces: The Seventeenth Century* (Leicester University Department of English Local History, *Occasional Papers*, 2d ser., no. 1, 1969), 15.

10. Bailyn, *Voyagers to the West: A Passage in the Peopling of America on the Eve of the Revolution* (New York, 1987), p. 376.

11. Robin Middleton, "The Sculpture Gallery at Newby Hall," *AA Files: Annals of the Architectural Association School of Architecture*, 13 (1986), 48–60; John Cornforth, "Newby Hall, North Yorkshire," *Country Life*, 165 (1979), 1802–06, 1918–21, 2006–09. For a detailed account, room by room, of Weddell's statuary collection and its acquisition, see Adolph Michaelis, *Ancient Marbles in Great Britain*, trans. C. A. M. Fennell (Cambridge, 1882), pp. 522–35; for the furnishings, Jill Low, "Newby Hall: Two Late Eighteenth-Century Inventories," *Furniture History*, 22 (1986), 140–65.

12. Middleton, "Sculpture Gallery," p. 59; Richard L. Morton, *Colonial Virginia* (Chapel Hill, N.C., 1960), II, 498; Thomas M. Doerflinger, *A Vigorous Spirit of Enterprise: Merchants and Economic Development in Revolutionary Philadelphia* (Chapel Hill, N.C., 1986), p. 134.

13. John Hayes, *Gainsborough: Paintings and Drawings* (London, 1975), p. 203; Ann Bermingham, *Landscape and Ideology: The English Rustic Tradition* (Berkeley, Calif., 1986), pp. 30–32.

14. For details of the Ellsworth portrait and the sitters' costumes, see Elizabeth M. Kornhauser, *Ralph Earl, the Face of the Young Republic* (New Haven, Conn., 1991), pp. 180–81; on the Sherman portrait, p. 109.

15. Adams to Abigail Adams, Philadelphia, March 16, 1777, in L. H. Butterfield et al., eds., *Adams Family Correspondence* (Cambridge, Mass., 1963–93), II, 176.

16. William Pierce (delegate from Georgia to the Philadelphia convention), "Character Sketches of Delegates," ed. Max Farrand, *Records of the Federal Convention of 1787* (rev. ed., New Haven, Conn., 1966), III, 88–89.

17. Bailyn, *Faces of Revolution*, pp. 28, 32.

18. For a detailed account of the experiences and attitudes of Americans traveling in Britain, their sense of alienation from the "homeland" (typically, John Dickinson: "I don't seem to have any connections with this country; I think myself only a traveller, & this the inn"; Henry Eustace

McCulloh: "I consider myself only as a sojourner in this land of Gomorrah"; Samuel Davies: I am "among strangers in a strange land"), see Susan Lindsey Lively, "Going Home: Americans in Britain, 1740–1776" (Ph.D. diss., Harvard University, 1997), quotations at p. 273.

19. Bailyn and John Clive, "England's Cultural Provinces: Scotland and America," *William and Mary Quarterly*, 3d ser., 11 (1954), 200–13. Cf. Richard B. Sher and Jeffrey R. Smitten, eds., *Scotland and America in the Age of Enlightenment* (Edinburgh, 1990). For David Hume's sensitivity to the Scottish "impurities" and "uncorrectness" in his speech and writing that reflected "a kind of cultural alienation from his own origins," see James G. Basker, "Scotticisms and the Problem of Cultural Identity in 18th Century Britain," in John Dwyer and Richard B. Sher, eds., *Sociability and Society in Eighteenth-Century Scotland (Eighteenth-Century Life,* 15, nos. 1–2 [1991]), 85.

20. Stevens, "Americanus" I (*Daily Advertiser* [New York], November 2, 1787), in Bailyn, ed., *The Debate on the Constitution* (New York, 1993), I, 228; Madison, *Federalist* No. 14, ibid., pp. 435–36.

21. Ellsworth, Speech in the Connecticut Ratifying Convention, January 7, 1788, in Bailyn, ed., *Debate,* I, 882–83 (emphasis added).

22. Stevens, "Americanus" I, in Bailyn, ed., *Debate,* I, 228; "Version of [James] Wilson's speech by Thomas Lloyd," November 24, 1787, in Merrill Jensen et al., eds., *The Documentary History of the Ratification of the Constitution* (Madison, Wisc., 1976–), II, 355.

23. Bailyn, *The Ideological Origins of the American Revolution* (enlarged ed., Cambridge, Mass., 1992), pp. 46–51, 86–92, 130–38; Madison, *Federalist* No. 51, in Bailyn, ed., *Debate,* II, 164; Madison's speech in the Virginia ratifying convention, June 20, 1788, in Jensen et al., *Documentary History,* X, 1417.

24. Madison, in *Federalist* No. 14, in Bailyn, ed., *Debate,* I, 436.

## CHAPTER II

1. Merrill D. Peterson, *The Jefferson Image in the American Mind* (New York, 1960), pp. 444, 443, 447, 279.

2. Merrill D. Peterson, *Adams and Jefferson: A Revolutionary Dialogue* ([1976] Oxford, 1978), p. 74; Leonard W. Levy, *Jefferson and Civil Liberties: The Darker Side* (Cambridge, Mass., 1963), p. 158; Peterson, "Henry Adams on Jefferson the President," *Virginia Quarterly Review,* 39 (1963), 192–93; Noble E. Cunningham, Jr., *In Pursuit of Reason: The Life of Thomas Jefferson* (Baton Rouge, La., 1987), p. 233; Harold C. Syrett et al., eds., *The Papers of Alexander Hamilton* (New York, 1961–79), XXV, 320.

3. Levy, *Jefferson and Civil Liberties,* pp. 160, 165; Michael Zuckerman, *Almost Chosen People . . .* (Berkeley, Calif., 1993), p. 196; Michael Lind, *The Next American Nation: The New Nationalism and the Fourth American Revolution* (New

York, 1995), pp. 369–71; Pauline Maier, *American Scripture: Making the Declaration of Independence* (New York, 1997), p. 150; Joseph J. Ellis, *American Sphinx: The Character of Thomas Jefferson* (New York, 1997), p. 299; Conor Cruise O'Brien, *The Long Affair: Thomas Jefferson and the French Revolution, 1785–1800* (Chicago, 1996), pp. 150, 310, 317 (cf. Bailyn, "Sally and Her Master," *Times Literary Supplement*, 4885 [Nov. 15, 1996], 3–4).

4. On Jefferson, slavery, and racism, see below, note 15; Levy, *Jefferson and Civil Liberties*, summary p. 18, details chaps. iii–vii.

5. Jeffrey L. Pasley, *"The Tyranny of Printers": Newspaper Politics in the Early American Republic* (Charlottesville, Va., 2001), traces in detail Jefferson's crucial role in founding partisan newspapers, encouraging, supporting, and indirectly managing them, from the early 1790s to at least 1814. The Republicans' "chief newspaper enthusiast," Pasley writes, Jefferson "repeatedly urged *other* Republican leaders to contribute editorially and financially to the party press." This summer, he wrote Madison in 1799, "is the season for systematic energies and sacrifices. The engine is the press. Every man must lay his purse and his pen under contribution" (p. 154).

On the Barbary pirates, Julian P. Boyd et al., eds., *The Papers of Thomas Jefferson* (Princeton, N.J., 1950–), VII, 512. On rebellions, ibid., XII, 356. On the Haitian rebellion, Zuckerman, *Almost Chosen People*, chap. vi. On Louisiana, Dumas Malone, *Jefferson and His Time* (Boston, 1948–81), IV, 316.

6. Malone, *Jefferson*, IV, 371; Cunningham, *Pursuit of Reason*, p. 139.

7. Malone, *Jefferson*, III, 341–45, chap. xxx.

8. Charles F. Adams, ed., *The Works of John Adams . . .* (Boston, 1850–56), II, 513–14. On Jefferson's role in the making of the Declaration: Maier, *American Scripture*, chap. iii.

9. Boyd et al., *Papers*, XI, 44; VIII, 404, 568–69.

10. Bailyn, *The Ideological Origins of the American Revolution* (enlarged ed., Cambridge, Mass., 1992), chaps. iii, iv.

11. For a summary of Jefferson's work as a minister in Paris, see Bailyn, *Faces of Revolution: Personalities and Themes in the Struggle for American Independence* (New York, 1990), pp. 35–39.

12. Noble E. Cunningham, Jr., *The Process of Government under Jefferson* (Princeton, N.J., 1978), pp. 317–19, 321; Cunningham, *The Jeffersonian Republicans in Power* (Chapel Hill, N.C., 1963), pp. 304–05.

13. Boyd et al., *Papers*, X, 50; XII, 440; XIV, 18–19; Bailyn, *Faces of Revolution*, p. 245; Malone, *Jefferson*, III, 401–05.

14. Malone, *Jefferson*, IV, 320.

15. Discussions of the controversial subject of Jefferson's racism and his views of slavery abound, many of them bitterly polemical. There are consid-

ered analyses in John C. Miller, *The Wolf by the Ears: Thomas Jefferson and Slavery* (New York, 1977); Winthrop D. Jordan, *White over Black . . .* (Chapel Hill, N.C., 1968), chap. xii; and Ellis, *American Sphinx,* pp. 144–52, 263–73, 303–07. The biological evidence of Jefferson's likely sexual relation with Sally Hemings has touched off a new wave of commentary on the complexity of his racism, which comes out clearly in the shift from the blatant views in his *Notes on the State of Virginia* ([1787] William H. Peden, ed., Chapel Hill, N.C., 1954), pp. 137–43, 162–63, to his letter to Henri Gregoire, written twenty years after the *Notes:* "Be assured that no person living wishes more sincerely than I do, to see a complete refutation of the doubts I have myself entertained and expressed on the grade of understanding alloted to them [Negroes] by nature, and to find that in this respect they are on a par with ourselves. My doubts were the result of personal observation on the limited sphere of my own State, where the opportunities for the development of their genius were not favorable, and those of exercising it still less so . . . they are gaining daily in the opinions of nations, and hopeful advances are making towards their reestablishment on an equal footing with the other colors of the human family" (February 25, 1809; Paul L. Ford, ed., *The Works of Thomas Jefferson* [New York, 1904–05], XI, 99–100). Cf. Annette Gordon-Reed, *Thomas Jefferson and Sally Hemings: An American Controversy* (Charlottesville, Va., 1997); Jan E. Lewis and Peter S. Onuf, eds., *Sally Hemings and Thomas Jefferson: History, Memory, and Civic Culture* (Charlottesville, Va., 1999); and Jan Lewis et al., "Thomas Jefferson and Sally Hemings Redux," *William and Mary Quarterly,* 3d ser., 57 (2000), 121–210.

16. Malone, *Jefferson,* VI, chap. xxiii.

17. Isaac Kramnick, *Bolingbroke and His Circle . . .* (Cambridge, Mass., 1968), chaps. ii, iii.

18. Ford, *Works,* I, 174, 177–80.

19. Ibid., X, 522; V, 11; *Notes on Virginia,* pp. 164–65; Malone, *Jefferson,* V, 620, 628; Ford, *Works,* XI, 504.

20. Donald F. Swanson, " 'Bank Notes Will Be But As Oak Leaves': Thomas Jefferson on Paper Money," *Virginia Magazine of History and Biography,* 101 (1993), 43; William D. Grampp, "A Re-examination of Jeffersonian Economics," *Southern Economic Journal,* 12 (1946), 263–82.

21. Boyd et al., *Papers,* IX, 239; Ford, *Works,* XI, 497; Boyd et al., *Papers,* XI, 49; Levy, *Jefferson and Civil Liberties,* 46; Ford, *Works,* X, 417.

22. For the three reforms of the Articles of Confederation that Jefferson advocated in the months before the Philadelphia convention (a general rule for admitting new states, a shift from property to population as the basis for federal taxation, and a stronger commerce clause), see Boyd et

al., *Papers*, X, 14–17. On Jefferson's responses to the Constitution, ibid., XII, 351, 440–41.

23. Ibid., XII, 446, 558, 569, 571; XIII, 208–09, 232, 378; XIV, 678.

24. Bailyn, *Ideological Origins*, chap. iii; Garrett W. Sheldon, *The Political Philosophy of Thomas Jefferson* (Baltimore, 1991), pp. 61–72, 143–45.

25. Boyd et al., *Papers*, X, 52.

26. Ibid., II, 526–35; Ford, *Works*, XI, 399; Henry A. Washington, ed., *The Writings of Thomas Jefferson . . .* (Washington, D.C., 1853–54), VII, 94–95; Ford, *Works*, XI, 523–24.

27. Washington, *Writings*, V, 608; Ford, *Works*, XII, 427; Cunningham, *Jeffersonian Republicans in Power*, p. 305.

28. Boyd et al., *Papers*, VIII, 681–82.

29. Ibid., I, 362.

30. Henry Adams, *History of the United States of America during the Second Administration of Thomas Jefferson* ([1890] New York, 1962), II, 281–82.

31. Malone, *Jefferson*, V, 667; Ford, *Works*, IX, 148.

CHAPTER III

1. Information on Gilbert's background and family is drawn from his autobiography, *A European Past: Memoirs, 1905–1945* (New York, 1988); from papers in the archives of the Institute for Advanced Study, especially notes by Patricia Labalme on Gilbert's early years in the United States and at the Institute; and from Hartmut Lehmann, ed., *Felix Gilbert as Scholar and Teacher* (German Historical Institute, *Occasional Paper*, no. 6, Washington, D.C., 1992).

2. Edward Mead Earle, head of the seminar, to Frank Aydelotte, Director of the Institute, July 5 and October 2, 1940, Archives of the Institute for Advanced Study.

3. After its initial publication by the Princeton University Press, *To the Farewell Address: Ideas of Early American Foreign Policy* was reprinted as a Harper Torchbook with the title *The Beginnings of American Foreign Policy* (1965). The substance of chapters ii and iii, developed directly from the papers Gilbert presented to the seminar, was published long before the book appeared: "The English Background of American Isolationism in the Eighteenth Century," *William and Mary Quarterly*, 3d ser., 1 (1944), 138–60; and "The 'New Diplomacy' of the Eighteenth Century," *World Politics*, 4 (1951), 1–38.

4. Gilbert, *To the Farewell Address*, pp. 6, 136.

5. Ibid., chaps. iii–v; quotation at p. 52.

6. James H. Hutson, *John Adams and the Diplomacy of the American Revolution* (Lexington, Ky., 1980); Hutson, "Intellectual Foundations of Early Amer-

ican Diplomacy," *Diplomatic History*, 1 (1977), 1–19; Alexander DeConde, "Historians, the War of American Independence, and the Persistence of the Exceptionalist Ideal," *International History Review*, 5 (1983), 399–430; Jonathan R. Dull, "American Foreign Relations before the Constitution: A Historiographical Wasteland," in Gerald K. Haines and J. Samuel Walker, eds., *American Foreign Relations: A Historiographical Review* (Westport, Conn., 1981), pp. 3–15; Dull, "Benjamin Franklin and the Nature of American Diplomacy," *International History Review*, 3 (1983), 346–63; Ronald Hoffman and Peter J. Albert, eds., *Diplomacy and Revolution: The Franco-American Alliance of 1778* (Charlottesville, Va., 1981): essays by Alexander DeConde and Lawrence S. Kaplan; William C. Stinchcombe, *The American Revolution and the French Alliance* (Syracuse, N.Y., 1969), chap. i; Gerald Stourzh, *Benjamin Franklin and American Foreign Policy* (Chicago, 1954), chap. iv (responding to Gilbert's two preliminary articles cited in note 3).

7. Bailyn, *Faces of Revolution: Personalities and Themes in the Struggle for American Independence* (New York, 1990), chap. i; Franklin to Robert R. Livingston, July 22, 1783: Francis Wharton, ed., *The Revolutionary Diplomatic Correspondence of the United States* (Washington, D.C., 1889), VI, 582. Within two months—on September 18—Franklin's comment on Adams was passed on to the Adamses by Elbridge Gerry: L. H. Butterfield et al., eds., *Adams Family Correspondence* (Cambridge, Mass., 1963–93), V, 250–52.

8. L. H. Butterfield et al., eds., *Diary and Autobiography of John Adams* (Cambridge, Mass., 1961), III, 418; Carl Van Doren, *Benjamin Franklin* (New York, 1938), pp. 367–72, 417–18 (quotation at 372); Claude-Anne Lopez, *Mon Cher Papa: Franklin and the Ladies of Paris* (New Haven, Conn., 1966); *The Works of John Adams . . .* (Charles F. Adams, ed., Boston, 1850–56), I, 660.

9. Butterfield et al., *Diary and Autobiography*, IV, 118; II, 391. By the time Adams returned to America, after a year of working with Franklin in Paris, his exasperation, mixed with envy of Franklin's social success, boiled over. Franklin, he wrote in his diary (May 10, 1779), "has a passion for reputation and fame, as strong as you can imagine, and his time and thoughts are chiefly employed to obtain it, and to set tongues and pens male and female, to celebrating him. Painters, statuaries, sculptors, china potters, and all are set to work for this end. He has the most affectionate and insinuating way of charming the woman or the man that he fixes on. It is the most silly and ridiculous way imaginable, in the sight of an American, but it succeeds, to admiration, fullsome and sickish as it is, in Europe." Ibid., II, 367.

10. Jonathan R. Dull, *Franklin the Diplomat: The French Mission* (*Transactions of the American Philosophical Society*, 72, part 1, 1982), chap. iv; Julian P. Boyd, "Silas Deane: Death by a Kindly Teacher of Treason?" *William and Mary*

*Quarterly*, 3d ser., 16 (1959), 176–87, 319–38; Leonard W. Labaree et al., eds., *The Papers of Benjamin Franklin* (New Haven, Conn., 1959–), XXIII, 211 (see also pp. 162, 414–15); XV, 22–25; Samuel F. Bemis, "British Secret Service and the French-American Alliance," *American Historical Review*, 29 (1924), 474–95; Butterfield et al., *Diary and Autobiography*, IV, 78. A more recent assessment of Adams's relation with Franklin in Paris stresses the initial amity between them and attributes Adams's growing suspicion and hostility to his increasing concern about the course of the war in late 1778. John Ferling, "John Adams, Diplomat," *William and Mary Quarterly*, 3d ser., 51 (1994), 234.

11. Dull, *Franklin the Diplomat*, pp. 26–32; Stourzh, *Franklin*, pp. 139–45; Boyd, "Deane," pp. 328–29.

12. Durand Echeverria, *Mirage in the West: A History of the French Image of American Society to 1815* (Princeton, N.J., 1957), chaps. i, ii.

13. Dull, *Franklin the Diplomat*, pp. 1–15; Bailyn, *Voyagers to the West: A Passage in the Peopling of America on the Eve of the Revolution* (New York, 1987), pp. 32–33; Van Doren, *Franklin*, pp. 383–87, 390, 419–21, 467–76; Mina J. Carson, "The London World of Benjamin Franklin" (MS seminar paper, Harvard University, 1979).

14. In the pages that follow, on the visual images of Franklin, I have relied heavily on Charles C. Sellers, *Benjamin Franklin in Portraiture* (New Haven, Conn., 1962). This masterly work is a guide to the technical complexity of Franklin's vast portraiture and the literature that surrounds it, and it is a commentary on both. Though I have used only some of Sellers's technical material in what follows, my general indebtedness to the book is profound. Unless otherwise noted, the background information, though not the interpretation, is drawn from Sellers's catalogue of the portraits.

15. Ibid., pp. 78–79.

16. Ibid., pp. 96–103.

17. Ibid., p. 374.

18. Keith Arbour has pointed out that the single word, so prominent and unexpected, may also have meant for Franklin, who relished puns, a subtle revenge for the public humiliation he had suffered four years earlier when England's solicitor general, Alexander Wedderburn, in the course of his blistering denunciation of him, had referred to him, in Latin, as a thief ("*fur*"): "One Last Word: Benjamin Franklin and the Duplessis Portrait of 1778," *Pennsylvania Magazine of History and Biography*, 118 (1994), 183–208. Arbour explains that the solicitor general, in that famous speech in the Privy Council chamber, mocked and slandered Franklin's reputation as a man of letters in a "triple Latin pun" by calling him "a man of *three* letters" ("*homo* trium *literarum*"), echoing Plautus's line: "You, a man of

three letters—thief [*fur*]." There is no evidence that contemporaries were aware of "*Vir*" on the portrait's frame as a "visual-literate" pun and hence a long-delayed and witty response to Wedderburn's insult, but that meaning is consistent with Franklin's interest in visual jokes, and consistent too with Franklin's wearing the same coat for the signing of the peace treaties with France in 1778 that he had worn that day in London when he had stood silent in the face of Wedderburn's tirade. If, as seems likely, the "baroque complexity" of the pun was intended, Franklin must have privately relished it for the rest of his days, whether anyone else was aware of the hidden reference or not. It is not likely, however, that, as Arbour also suggests, Franklin's wearing a coat with a *fur* collar in the Duplessis portrait was a further reinforcement of the pun, if only because he wore fur-fringed coats in other portraits.

19. *Chronique de Paris,* June 17, 1790.
20. Echeverria, *Mirage in the West,* p. 57.
21. Ibid., p. 58; Butterfield et al., *Diary and Autobiography,* IV, 80–81. The two venerable *philosophes* left the room to great public applause, having demonstrated, the *Journal de Paris* reported on May 1, "une amitié si touchante entre deux hommes qui, à deux milles lieues l'un de l'autre, ont consacré leur vie au même objet, l'accroissement des lumières et le bonheur du genre humain"; Labaree et al., *Papers of Franklin,* XXVI, 362n. In July 1778 the Lodge of the Nine Sisters presented Franklin with Helvétius's apron, which had been worn by the recently deceased Voltaire; in 1779 and 1780 Franklin was elected Grand Master; ultimately, after many other celebrations of Franklin as a statesman and benefactor of humanity, the Lodge offered a prize for the best eulogy of Franklin.
22. Stourzh, *Franklin,* pp. 139–45.
23. Bailyn, *The Ideological Origins of the American Revolution* (enlarged edition, Cambridge, Mass., 1992), postscript ("Fulfillment: A Commentary on the Constitution").
24. Ibid., pp. 349–51.

## CHAPTER IV

1. John C. Hamilton, ed., *The Federalist* (Philadelphia, 1864), pp. lxxxviii–lxxxix; Benjamin F. Wright, "*The Federalist* on the Nature of Political Man," *Ethics,* 59 (1949), 3; Merrill Jensen et al., eds., *The Documentary History of the Ratification of the Constitution* (Madison, Wisc., 1976–), XIII, 493; XV, 521 (hereafter: *Documentary History*).
2. Robert A. Rutland, "The First Great Newspaper Debate: The Constitutional Crisis of 1787–88," *Proceedings of the American Antiquarian Society,* 97, part 1 (1987), 53.

3. Elizabeth Fleet, ed., "Madison's 'Detached Memoranda,'" *William and Mary Quarterly*, 3d ser., 3 (1946), 565; Linda G. De Pauw, *The Eleventh Pillar: New York State and the Federal Constitution* (Ithaca, N.Y., 1966), p. 109; Thomas S. Engeman et al., eds., *The* Federalist *Concordance* ([Middletown, Conn.], 1980), pp. [xi]–xiii; Julian P. Boyd et al., eds., *The Papers of Thomas Jefferson* (Princeton, N.J., 1950–), XIII, 499; Douglass Adair, *Fame and the Founding Fathers* (New York, 1974), pp. 54–55; William T. Hutchinson et al., eds., *The Papers of James Madison* (Chicago, 1962–), X, 259, 261. For an example of differences between Madison and Hamilton on a vital issue, see William B. Allen, "Federal Representation: The Design of the Thirty-fifth *Federalist* Paper," *Publius*, 6 (1976), 66–67. J. Q. Adams's remark refers to differences between Hamilton's *Federalist* No. 9 and Madison's No. 10.

4. Jacob E. Cooke, ed., *The Federalist* (Middletown, Conn., 1961), p. xiv; Hamilton, *Federalist*, pp. lxxxv–lxxxvi; Adair, *Fame,* pp. 53, 57; De Pauw, *Eleventh Pillar,* p. 109. On the sources for *Federalist* No. 10: Hutchinson et al., *Madison Papers*, X, 205–19, IX, 348–57; on the sources for Nos. 18–20: ibid., pp. 4–22. (All references below to *The Federalist* are to the Cooke edition; paper numbers are followed, where relevant, by page numbers.)

5. See above, "A Note on the *The Federalist* and the Supreme Court," pp. 126–30. For an elaborate discussion of the "textualists'" (especially Justice Scalia's) reliance on *The Federalist* in constitutional cases, several of the justices' disagreements in interpreting specific numbers of *The Federalist,* and the theoretical issues involved in the use of the papers in contemporary jurisprudence, see John F. Manning, "Textualism and Original Understanding . . . the Role of the Federalist in Constitutional Adjudication," and William N. Eskridge, Jr., "Textualism and Original Understanding. . . ," both in *George Washington Law Review,* 66 (June/August 1998).

6. William E. Gladstone, "Kin Beyond Sea," *North American Review,* 127 (1878), 185.

7. The full documentation of the struggle over the ratification of the Constitution is being edited and published at the University of Wisconsin (note 1, above), where John P. Kaminski, Gaspare J. Saladino, and their assistants are carrying on the work begun by Merrill Jensen. The sixteen volumes published so far include not only the texts of the formal debates in the ratifying conventions but letters, pamphlets, news items, newspaper polemics, and relevant ephemera of all kinds. Bailyn, ed., *The Debate on the Constitution* (2 vols., New York, 1993), is a selected edition of this vast archive, including both formal speeches and the arguments and polemics on both sides of the issues. (Cited hereafter as *Debate.*)

8. The "Brutus" essays were first republished in full in William Jeffrey, Jr., ed., "The Letters of 'Brutus'—A Neglected Element in the Ratification

Campaign of 1787–88," *Cincinnati Law Review*, 40, no. 4 (1971), 643–777. All
but two of the papers (Nos. 2 and 16) are reprinted in *Debate*, I, II.

9. For the wilder excesses of the polemics, see Bailyn, *Faces of Revolution:
Personalities and Themes in the Struggle for American Independence* (New York,
1990), pp. 233–34. The Constitution that emerged from Philadelphia,
Madison wrote in 1796, was nothing more than "the draft of a plan,
nothing but a dead letter, until life and validity were breathed into it by
the voice of the people, speaking through the several State Conventions.
If we were to look, therefore, for the meaning of the instrument beyond
the face of the instrument, we must look for it, not in the General Convention, which proposed, but in the State Conventions, which accepted
and ratified the Constitution." Madison, Speech in Congress, April 6,
1796, in Gaillard Hunt, ed., *The Writings of James Madison* (New York,
1900–10), VI, 272.

10. Bailyn, *The Ideological Origins of the American Revolution* (enlarged ed., Cambridge, Mass., 1992), chaps. i–iii.

11. *Debate*, II, 906.

12. "Brutus" V, VI, in *Debate*, I, 503, 617. On the fear of the treaty-making
power: ibid., 275–76, 348; II, 569, 747–48. On the fear of the powers of an
"aristocratical" Senate: ibid., I, 60–61, 85–87, 115, 401; II, 881. William
Symmes, Jr., to Peter Osgood, Jr., Nov. 15, 1787, in *Documentary History*, XIV,
111; Luther Martin, "The Genuine Information," IX, in *Debate*, I, 654–55.

13. Bailyn, *Faces of Revolution*, pp. 237–38, 245–46; *Documentary History*, X, 1317,
1321–22; Caleb Wallace to William Fleming, Locust Groves, Ky., May 3,
1788, ibid., IX, 782; "Brutus" VIII, in *Debate*, I, 732.

14. Hamilton, *Federalist* No. 30, p. 193.

15. Hamilton, *Federalist* No. 29, p. 185; No. 84, p. 582; David Caldwell, Speech
in the North Carolina convention, in Jonathan Elliot, ed., *Debates in the Several State Conventions on the Adoption of the Federal Constitution* . . . (2d ed.,
Washington, D.C., 1836–45), IV, 62 (emphasis added); Madison, *Federalist*
No. 43, p. 295.

16. Madison, *Federalist* No. 45, pp. 311–14; Hamilton, *Federalist* No. 29, pp.
181 ff. ("a well regulated militia [is] the most natural defence of a free
country"—p. 182).

17. See especially Hamilton, *Federalist* Nos. 8 and 26, pp. 44 ff., 164 ff.; quotations at p. 169.

18. Patrick Henry, Speech in the Virginia convention, June 7, 1788, *Documentary History*, IX, 1046; Madison, *Federalist* No. 39, pp. 251–55; *Federalist* No.
49, p. 339.

19. Hamilton, *Federalist* Nos. 12, 36, pp. 75–76, 225–29.

20. Madison, *Federalist* No. 41, pp. 276–78.

21. Hamilton, *Federalist* No. 35, pp. 219–21; Madison, *Federalist* No. 10, pp. 62–63. For extended discussions of this complex subject, see Allen, "Federal Representation," pp. 61–71; Jack N. Rakove, *Original Meanings: Politics and Ideas in the Making of the Constitution* (New York, 1996), chap. viii.

22. Madison, *Federalist* No. 51, p. 353; *Federalist* No. 10, p. 64; *Federalist* Nos. 47–51.

23. Hamilton, *Federalist* No. 84, pp. 576–80.

24. Hamilton, *Federalist* Nos. 32, 33, esp. pp. 202–03.

25. Madison, *Federalist* No. 51, p. 349.

26. Madison to Jefferson, October 24, 1787, in Hutchinson et al., *Papers of James Madison*, X, 206–19 (for his "digression" on the need for "a check on the states," pp. 209–14); Madison, *Federalist* Nos. 10; 43, pp. 293–94; 51, pp. 351–52; Madison, Speech in the Virginia convention, June 6, 1788, *Debate*, II, 612.

27. Madison, *Federalist* No. 55, p. 378 (cf. Madison, Speech in the Virginia convention, [June 19 or 20, 1788] [in response to Mason on Article III], in Elliot, *Debates in the Several State Conventions*, III, 536–37); Hamilton, *Federalist* No. 76, pp. 513–14.

28. Madison to Edward Livingston, Montpelier, April 17, 1824, *Letters and Other Writings of James Madison . . .* (Philadelphia, 1865), III, 435–36.

29. *McCulloch v. Maryland* (1819); Herbert A. Johnson et al., eds., *The Papers of John Marshall* (Chapel Hill, N.C., 1974–), VIII, 259–80, 345–63.

30. These numbers, based on the LEXIS Academic Universe database, differ only slightly from the study of Ira C. Lupu, "Time, the Supreme Court, and *The Federalist*," *George Washington Law Review*, 66 (1998), 1324–36. See also Lupu, "The Most-Cited *Federalist* Papers," *Constitutional Commentary*, 15 (1998), 403–10. I thank Prof. Noah Feldman for guidance in this bibliography.

31. Lee Epstein et al., eds., *The Supreme Court Compendium . . .* , 2d ed. (Washington, D.C., 1996), pp. 84–85. See above, chap. iv, n. 5.

32. *Scott v. Sandford* (1857); *Printz v. U.S.* (1997).

CHAPTER V

I am grateful to Professor George A. Billias, of Clark University, for allowing me to read the manuscript of his work-in-progress, *Heard Round the World*. His documentation of responses to American constitutionalism abroad under major headings—federalism, presidentialism, judicial review, etc.—when completed will be the major work on the subject. For a preliminary survey, see his essay in *American Constitutionalism Abroad*, cited below, note 7.

1. Abbé Raynal, *The Revolution of America* (2d edition, Philadelphia, 1782), p. 41. This work was originally published in French as Book 18, chaps. xxxviii–lii in the third edition of *Histoire philosophique et politique des établissemens et du commerce des Européens dans les deux Indes* (Geneva, 1780). It appeared as a separate pamphlet in 1781 in both English (first edition printed in London, translator not indicated) and French. For the numerous reprintings, see the entries in Durand Echeverria and Everett C. Wilkie, Jr., eds., *The French Image in America . . . Bibliography . . .* (2 vols., Metuchen, N.J., and London, 1994), especially I, 470–71.

2. Charles Maurice Camille de Talleyrand-Perigord, *Étude sur la république des États-Unis d'Amérique* (New York, 1876), p. 192; John C. Hamilton, ed., *The Federalist* (Philadelphia, 1864), p. lxxxviii; Franklin D. Scott, *The United States and Scandinavia* (Cambridge, Mass., 1950), pp. 65–66; Richard B. Morris, *The Emerging Nations and the American Revolution* (New York, 1979), pp. 95–96; Hartmut Lehmann, "The Positions of Rulers in Eighteenth-Century Germany and America," in Hermann Wellenreuther, ed., *German and American Constitutional Thought: Contexts, Interaction, and Historical Realities* (New York, 1990), pp. 161–62.

3. Kenneth Maxwell, "The Impact of the American Revolution on Spain and Portugal and Their Empires," in Jack P. Greene and J. R. Pole, eds., *The Blackwell Encyclopedia of the American Revolution* (Cambridge, Mass., and Oxford, 1991), p. 534; Julian Boyd et al., eds., *The Papers of Thomas Jefferson* (Princeton, N.J., 1950–), X, 427, 546–47, 636–37, XI, 20, 225, 339–41; Júnia Furtado, "Mirror of the World: Libertines, Heretics, and the Rebellious in Baroque Minas Gerais, Brazil . . ." (Working Paper, International Seminar on the History of the Atlantic World, 1500–1825, Harvard University, 2001), p. 3 (see also Kenneth Maxwell, *Conflicts and Conspiracies: Brazil and Portugal, 1750–1808* [Cambridge, 1973], pp. 80–83); Friedrich von Gentz, "Der Ursprung und die Grundsätze der Amerikanischen Revolution, verglichen mit dem Ursprunge und den Grundsätze der Französischen," *Historisches Journal* (May 1800), translated by John Quincy Adams as *The Origin and Principles of the American Revolution, Compared with the Origin and Principles of the French Revolution* (Philadelphia, 1800); William S. Robertson, *Hispanic-American Relations with the United States* (New York, 1923), pp. 70–71.

4. *The Crisis*, August 24, 1776, no. 84. The first French translation was probably the one printed by the *Gazette de Leyde* (*Nouvelles politiques publiées à Leyde, ou Nouvelles extraordinaires de divers endroits* is its proper title) on August 30, 1776, followed by the *Journal historique et politique* on September 10. Durand Echeverria, "French Publications of the Declaration of Independence and the American Constitutions, 1776–1783," *Papers of the Bibliographic Soci-*

*ety of America,* 47 (1953), 322; Elise Marienstras and Naomi Wulf, "French
Translations and Reception of the Declaration of Independence," *Jour-
nal of American History,* 85 (1999), 1304–06; Willi Paul Adams, "German
Translations of the American Declaration of Independence," ibid., pp.
1331–32; [Matthias Christian Sprengel], *Briefe den gegenwärtigen Zustand von
Nord America betreffend* (Göttingen, 1777), p. 52.

5. Echeverria, "French Publications," pp. 323–26. The version of the Articles of Confederation that Franklin brought with him and had translated
was the second draft (August 1776) of which only eighty copies were
printed, one for each member of the Congress; the printer was sworn to
secrecy, since Congress wished to keep the text confidential until they
were ready to submit a final draft to the states for ratification. It differed
significantly from the final version of 1777 (adopted 1781) and could only
have misled French readers on the weakness of the union that was evolving in America. It did not pledge the states to assume the charges that
Congress had incurred, as the final version would, nor did it have the all-
important interstate "privileges and immunities" and "full faith and
credit" clauses which would bind the states into a legal unit (and would be
carried over verbatim into the federal Constitution), nor did it guarantee
free travel or commerce among the states without invidious duties or
other impositions. Cf. Jack N. Rakove, *The Beginnings of National Politics*
(New York, 1979), pp. 180–81.

6. John Almon published the serial *The Remembrancer; or, Impartial Repository of
Public Events* in London from 1775 to 1784. La Rochefoucauld and Franklin
worked together to publish the series *Affaires de l'Angleterre et de l'Amérique*
(1776–1779), listed as Antwerp but actually published in Paris. Although no
editor or translator is listed on the title page of the *Recueil des lois constitutives
des colonies anglaises* . . . (Paris, 1778), the dedication page (a tribute to
Franklin) is signed "Regnier," and Gilbert Chinard has attributed the edi-
torship to this anonymous Regnier. Many assume that Regnier was La
Rochefoucauld. Chinard, "Notes on the French Translations of the
'Forms of Government or Constitutions of the Several United States' 1778
and 1783," *Year Book of the American Philosophical Society,* 1943, 88–106; Echeverria, "French Publications," pp. 317–18; Marienstras and Wulf, "French
Translations," pp. 1304–05. Quote from the *Recueil* dedication page.

7. Franklin to Samuel Cooper, Paris, May 1, 1777, Leonard W. Labaree et al.,
eds., *Papers of Benjamin Franklin* (New Haven, Conn., 1959–), XXIV, 6. The
Constitution appeared in French translation in the *Gazette de Leyde* on
November 13, 1787, and in the *Journal Politique de Bruxelles,* part on November
17, 1787, and the rest on November 24. In Paris it appeared in early 1788 in
Filipo Mazzei's *Recherches historiques et politiques sur les États-Unis* . . . (4 vols.,

Paris, 1788) and it appeared in German in Johann Wilhelm von Archen-
holtz's *English Lyceum*, part in October and part in December. Horst Dippel,
*Germany and the American Revolution, 1770–1800* . . . , trans. Bernhard A. Uhlen-
dorf (Chapel Hill, N.C., 1977), p. 29; Jan W. S. Nordholt, *The Dutch Republic
and American Independence*, trans. Herbert H. Rowen (Chapel Hill, N.C., 1982),
pp. 118–19; *Staatsgesetze der dreyzehn vereinigten amerikanischen Staaten. Aus dem
Franzosischen übersetzt* (Dessau, 1785); Gottfried Dietze, *The Federalist: A Classic
on Federalism and Free Government* ([1960] Westport, Conn., 1977), p. 10. Miguel
de Pombo also translated the Constitution, the Declaration, and the Articles
and printed them in a two-hundred-page booklet in Bogotá. In early 1813, a
Spanish translation of the entire U.S. Constitution was in the possession of
prominent leaders of the Paraguayan revolution: Robertson, *Hispanic-
American Relations*, pp. 70–71, 75, 80, 83, 84; Robert J. Kolesar, "North American Constitutionalism and Spanish America . . . ," in George A. Billias, ed.,
*American Constitutionalism Abroad: Selected Essays in Comparative Constitutional His-
tory* (New York, 1990), pp. 47–48.

8. Robert R. Palmer, *The Age of Democratic Revolution* (Princeton, N.J., 1959), I,
   282.

9. Bailyn, *Faces of Revolution: Personalities and Themes in the Struggle for American
   Independence* (New York, 1990), pp. 155–56; Price, *Observations on the Importance of the American Revolution* (London, 1784), in which Price included
   Turgot's letter stating that Franklin had given him the first pamphlet,
   pp. 71–87.

10. Palmer, *Age of Democratic Revolution*, I, 269–70. On Adams's *Defence*: C.
    Bradley Thompson, *John Adams and the Spirit of Liberty* (Lawrence, Kans.,
    1998), especially chap. v.

11. [John Stevens], *Observations on Government, Including Some Animadversions on
    Mr. Adams's Defence of the Constitutions of Government of the United States of
    America* . . . (New York, 1787), pp. [3], 6, 28, 46, 50. The translation into
    French appeared under the title *Examen du gouvernement d'Angleterre comparé
    aux constitutions des États-Unis* . . . (Paris, 1789). See Palmer, *Age of Democratic
    Revolution*, I, 279–82, for the identification of the translators and a discus-
    sion of the pamphlet's importance in France.

12. Condorcet, "Quatre Lettres d'un bourgeois de New-Heaven [Haven]
    . . . ," in *Recherches historiques*, reprinted in Condorcet's *Oeuvres* (A. Con-
    dorcet O'Connor and M. F. Arago, eds., Paris, 1847–49), IX, 1–93; Mazzei,
    *Researches on the United States* (trans. and ed. Constance D. Sherman, Char-
    lottesville, Va., 1976), pp. 139–40; Palmer, *Age of Democratic Revolution*, I, 279.

13. Arthur Sheps, "The American Revolution and the Transformation of
    English Republicanism," *Historical Reflections = Réflexions historiques*, 10 (1975),
    3, 6, 26–28.

14. Henry E. Bourne, "American Constitutional Precedents in the French National Assembly," *American Historical Review*, 8 (1903), 474–85; J. Salwyn Schapiro, *Condorcet and the Rise of Liberalism* ([1934] New York, 1963), p. 221; Palmer, *Age of Democratic Revolution*, I, 489–502; Joyce Appleby, "America as a Model for the Radical French Reformers of 1789," *William and Mary Quarterly*, 3d ser., 28 (1971), 275–86.

15. William E. Rappard, "Pennsylvania and Switzerland: The American Origins of the Swiss Constitution," in *Studies in Political Science and Sociology* (Philadelphia, 1941), pp. 56, 70, 78, 93.

16. Brian R. Hamnett, "Process and Pattern: A Re-examination of the Ibero-American Independence Movements, 1808–1826," *Journal of Latin American Studies*, 29 (1977), 282–83, 287, 321–22, 326; Timothy E. Anna, "Disintegration Is in the Eye of the Beholder: Mexican Federalism and Early Nationhood, 1821–1835," in Anthony McFarlane and Eduardo Posada-Carbó, eds., *Independence and Revolution in Spanish America: Perspectives and Problems* (London, 1999), pp. 182–83.

17. Kolesar, "North American Constitutionalism and Spanish America," pp. 41, 49; J. B. Trend, *Bolivar and the Independence of Spanish America* (London, 1946), p. 94; Robertson, *Hispanic-American Relations*, p. 86; Victor A. Belaunde, *Bolivar and the Political Thought of the Spanish American Revolution* (Baltimore, 1938), pp. 174–75.

18. Kolesar, "North American Constitutionalism and Spanish America," pp. 50–51; John Lynch, *The Spanish American Revolutions, 1808–1826* (New York, 1973), pp. 146–47, 104, 324; Robertson, *Hispanic-American Relations*, pp. 81, 84–86, 64–66; Joedd Price, "Images and Influences: The Legacy of the Founding Fathers and the Federal System in Ecuador," *Latin American Research Review*, 10 (1975), 128–29; Hamnett, "Process and Pattern," p. 324; cf. Charles A. Hale, *Mexican Liberalism in the Age of Mora, 1821–1853* (New Haven, Conn., 1968), chap. vi.

19. Lynch, *Spanish American Revolutions*, p. 66; Hamnett, "Process and Pattern," pp. 323–24; Gustavo L. Paz, " 'The Rights of the *Pueblos*': The Emergence of the First Sovereignties in Argentina's Revolution for Independence" (Working Paper, International Seminar on the History of the Atlantic World, 1500–1825, Harvard University, 2001), esp. p. 15; Kolesar, "North American Constitutionalism and Spanish America," pp. 52–55.

20. Gottfried Dietze, "Robert von Mohl, Germany's de Tocqueville," in Dietze, ed., *Essays on the American Constitution* (Englewood Cliffs, N.J., 1964), p. 192; Prof. Maximilian Schele De Vere, quoted in Billias, *Heard Round the World* (forthcoming), chap. xi, sect. 2; cf. Carl J. Friedrich, *The Impact of American Constitutionalism Abroad* (Boston, 1967), esp. pp. 52–55.

21. Eugene Curtis, *The French Assembly of 1848 and American Constitutional Doctrines* (Columbia Univ., *Studies in History, Economics, and Public Law*, LXXIX, no. 2, 1918).

22. Ibid., p. 152; Condorcet, "The Influence of the American Revolution in Europe," trans. Durand Echeverria, *William and Mary Quarterly*, 3d ser., 25 (1968), 93; Dumas Malone, *Jefferson and His Time* (Boston, 1948–81), V, 667.

# Illustration Credits

p. 21 Joshua Reynolds, *Prince William Augustus, Duke of Cumberland.* Devonshire Collection, Chatsworth, England. Reproduced by permission of the Duke of Devonshire and the Chatsworth Settlement Trustees.

p. 21 Thomas Gainsborough, *Georgiana, Duchess of Devonshire.* Courtesy, National Gallery of Art, Washington, D.C., Andrew W. Mellon Collection.

p. 22 John Downman, *Portrait of the Earl of Hillsborough.* Courtesy, the Marquess of Salisbury.

p. 22 Gainsborough, *Mary, Countess Howe.* Courtesy, the Iveagh Bequest, Kenwood House, London.

pp. 23–24 Gainsborough, *Mr. and Mrs. Andrews, Mr. and Mrs. William Hallett, and John Plampin.* Courtesy, National Gallery, London.

pp. 26–27 Ralph Earl, *Portrait of Oliver Ellsworth and Abigail Wolcott Ellsworth,* 1792. Courtesy, Wadsworth Atheneum Museum of Art, gift of the Ellsworth Heirs.

p. 28 Earl, *Roger Sherman (1791–1793).* Courtesy, Yale University Art Gallery, gift of Roger Sherman White B.A. 1899, LL.B. 1902.

p. 29 Chauncey B. Ives, *Statue of Roger Sherman.* National Statuary Hall, United States Capitol. Courtesy, the Architect of the Capitol.

### IMAGES OF BENJAMIN FRANKLIN

p. 70 Portrait by Robert Feke, ca. 1746. Courtesy, Harvard University Portrait Collection, bequest of Dr. John Collins Warren. Copyright, President and Fellows of Harvard College.

p. 71 George Dunlop Leslie, copy of a portrait by Mason Chamberlin, 1762. Courtesy, Yale University Art Gallery, gift of Avery Rockefeller.

p. 72 Portrait by David Martin. Courtesy, the White House, Washington, D.C.

p. 74 Engraving by Augustin de Saint-Aubin, after a drawing by Charles Nicolas Cochin, the Younger, 1777. Courtesy, Franklin Collection, Yale University Library.

p. 76 *Top left:* Jean-Jacques Rousseau, mezzotint by David Martin, 1766, after the painting by Allan Ramsay. Courtesy, the British Museum. *Top right:* Trial terra-cotta medallion by Jean Baptiste Nini, after a drawing by Thomas Walpole, 1777. Courtesy, Mr. Richard Margolis, Teaneck, N.J.
*Bottom:* Terra-cotta medallion by Jean Baptiste Nini, after a drawing by Thomas Walpole, 1777. Courtesy, Fogg Art Museum, Harvard

University, gift of Grenville L. Winthrop. Photo by Michael Nedzweski. Copyright, President and Fellows of Harvard College.

*p. 77*  Franklin portrait medallion on Sèvres coffee cup, with saucer, ca. 1779. Courtesy, Hillwood Museum, Washington, D.C.

*p. 78*  Statuette group, porcelain, Louis XVI and Franklin, by Lemire (Charles Gabriel Sauvage), ca. 1785. Courtesy, Winterthur Museum.

*p. 79*  *Franklin Experimenting.* Painted model, composition and wood, in glass case, 1780(?). Courtesy, Musée d'Art et d'Histoire, St. Germain-en-Laye, France/Bridgeman Art Library.

*p. 80*  Polychromed wax high relief attributed to Bernhardt Kaspar Hardy, Cologne, ca. 1785–95. Courtesy, PMVP/Toumazet.

*p. 81*  Terra-cotta statuette attributed to François-Marie Suzanne, 1793. Courtesy, The Walters Art Museum, Baltimore.

*p. 82*  Terra-cotta bust by Jean-Jacques Caffiéri, 1777. Courtesy, Centre des Monuments Nationaux, Paris.

*p. 83*  Marble bust by Jean-Antoine Houdon, 1778. Courtesy, The Metropolitan Museum of Art, gift of John Bard, 1872.

*p. 85*  *Le Docteur Franklin Couronné par la Liberté.* Aquatint by the Abbé de Saint-Non, after a drawing by Jean-Honoré Fragonard, 1778. Courtesy, Philadelphia Museum of Art, gift of Mrs. John D. Rockefeller, Jr.

*p. 86*  *Eripuit Coelo Fulmen, Sceptrumque Tirannis / Au Genie de Franklin.* Etching by Marguerite Gérard, after a design by Jean-Honoré Fragonard, 1778. Courtesy, Franklin Collection, Yale University Library.

*p. 87*  *L'Amérique Indépendante / Dediée au Congrès des États unis de l'Amérique.* Engraving by Charles Le Vasseur, after a drawing by Antoine Borel, 1778. Courtesy, Philadelphia Museum of Art, gift of Mrs. John D. Rockefeller, Jr., 1946.

*p. 88*  *Top:* Portrait by Charles Amédée Philippe Van Loo, ca. 1777–85. Courtesy, American Philosophical Society.
*Bottom:* Portrait by Pierre-Michel Alix, ca. 1790. Courtesy, Philadelphia Museum of Art, gift of Mrs. John D. Rockefeller, Jr., 1946.

*p. 89*  Pastel portrait by Jean-Baptiste Greuze, 1777. Courtesy, Diplomatic Reception Rooms, U.S. Department of State, Washington, D.C.

*p. 90*  Miniature in enamel by Jacques Thouron, ca. 1789. Courtesy, Réunion des Musées Nationaux/Art Resource, New York.

*p. 91*  Engraving by Louis Jacques Cathelin, after the painting by Anne-Rosalie Filleul, 1779. Courtesy, Franklin Collection, Yale University Library.

*p. 93*  Portrait by Joseph Siffred Duplessis, 1778. Courtesy, The Metropoli-

tan Museum of Art, the Friedsam Collection, bequest of Michael
Friedsam, 1931. (32.100.132) Photograph © 1981 The Metropolitan
Museum of Art.

*p. 94*  *L'Apotre de la Liberté Immortalisé,* drawn and engraved by Barincou
Monbrun, ca. 1790. Courtesy, American Philosophical Society.

*p. 95*  *Mirabeau Arrive aux Champs Éliseés,* engraved by L. J. Masquelier after
J. M. Moreau the Younger, ca. 1791. Courtesy, American Philosophical Society.

# Acknowledgments

In the preparation of this book I have had help initially by Barbara DeWolfe and more recently by Ginger Hawkins, who tracked down bibliographies and documents and checked details with skill and ingenuity. I am grateful to both of them, to Kirstie S. Venanzi of the Institute for Advanced Study, who handled negotiations with the custodians of French archives for permission to use illustrations in their care, and to Professor Jack Rakove, who alerted me to several questions of detail. My old friend and editor Jane Garrett, in this case as in others, has shown wonderful patience and fine judgment.

The preliminary versions of these essays, now much revised and expanded, were presented at conferences and published by the sponsors. I am grateful to them for the opportunities they offered me and for their help and hospitality on the occasion of the presentations: I, the National Endowment of the Humanities (the Jefferson Lecture); II, the American Philosophical Society; III, the Institute for Advanced Study; IV, the Library of Congress; V, the Institute of United States Studies, University of London.

# Index

Page numbers in *italics* refer to illustrations.